God's Got The Pen

REMEMBERING WHO I AM AND WHY I'M HERE — AGAIN

Steve Johnson

ISBN: 9781694314284
Imprint: Independently published

Typeset by Amnet Systems.
Cover design by Amnet Systems.

The feather flew, not because of anything in itself, but because the air bore it along. Thus am I *a feather on the breath of God.*
—Hildegard of Bingen

Table of Contents

Author's Note

SOME OF THE experiences I describe in this book are mysterious. You may find them unbelievable. So be it. I don't write to convince you of anything. I'm just telling my story.

There are a great many people who helped me get to this place in this life. I'm eternally grateful to all of you. This book is in many ways the product of your handiwork.

Introduction

As a kid, I watched the adults around me. I listened to what they said, most of the time. I tried to live the way they lived. Like those who came before me and those around me, I learned the right way to live. Folks called it the American Dream.

I went to work on it: get a good education, get a good job, get a picture-perfect family, get a nice house and a nice car and a lot of stuff, get a better job, then a bigger house and a nicer car and more stuff, get your children good educations, and get them cars too, eat at fancy restaurants and take vacations in sunny places, go to charity dinners and eat chicken, give a bit of money to the needy, send your kids off to college, retire, move to the country, live on a farm, check your bank account occasionally, wait for grandchildren and spoil them for a while before you die.

Suddenly I was 60 years old and I'd checked all the boxes except the ones marked *grandchildren* and *die*. According to family and friends, I'd done it. I'd mostly lived my life the right way. They smiled and congratulated me. I smiled back and thanked them, but inside I felt empty. I knew there was more to this life and it didn't seem to be where I was.

One day I noticed a voice. It wasn't like any of the usual voices in my head. It was soft and loving—definitely not one of the usual voices.

Time to go, the voice said. *God got da pen.* It was a surprising message wrapped in poor grammar.

I heard *time to go* repeated in quiet moments day and night for the next couple of months. I resisted and then, surprising everybody including myself, I walked away from the life I'd worked so hard to do right. I walked away from family, friends and stuff accumulated over a lifetime.

As you'd imagine, people were not happy with me. They felt abandoned. They lectured me about living the right way which, according to them, suddenly I wasn't.

I understood them sometimes. Sometimes I agreed with them. But every time I looked back (and I looked back a lot), I knew there was no going back. So I walked on—through the anger, through the loneliness, through the doubt, through it all, one foot in front of the other, wondering what the hell I was doing, my stomach in knots, hoping time and space would do their good work.

As I walked, I came to know myself differently. I loosened up and slowed down enough to listen—unusual for me—and that opened the door to a daily conversation with God and a host of unseen helpers. Call them what you like—angels, muses, whatever. They don't seem to care about labels. Not all that long ago you'd have said I was the least likely person on the planet to talk with God or chat with angels and you'd have been close to right, but that's what I do now. Things change.

Through quiet listening, dreams more real than reality, my paintings (think finger-painting), regular journaling (mostly not all that interesting), and my experience of the baffling mystery that surrounds us all, I have come to understand some things.

There is a vast invisible realm beyond what I see. My human perspective is shrouded in deep fog. I've discovered I don't know much, not much at all, not nearly as much as I thought I knew. As a consequence, I've slowly let go of beliefs and judgments about a lot of things.

I am both messy human and divine being—a God spark. I'm just like you.

I bring my spark to light a fire with a new energy that pulses through me. (Nobody's more surprised by that than I am.) Like electric current, I feel it running through me day and night. I'm told it triggers apotheosis and ignites the apocalypse. That bit of news sounded ominous until I looked the words up. Apotheosis is the blooming of individual divinity. The apocalypse is the lifting of the veil between heaven and earth. Sounds alright, doesn't it?

The new energy moves through me and goes where it's needed. Like raindrops on the surface of a pond, it ripples out with each pulse in ever-growing circles, but instead of diminishing, the ripples grow larger and more powerful. At some point, they touch us all.

For delivery of this gift, I'm connected to eight of my previous lives (more about this later). They are a growing part of me. They remind me who I am and why I've come back. They are important to the flow of energy.

Others are bringing their gifts too. I'm not the only one. We each have a gift to bring. You'll step forward and tell your story if you choose to. I speak only for myself.

The way of apotheosis isn't easy. It's an exercise in personal responsibility—our individual ability to respond to each moment in love for ourselves, others and the Earth. It offers us the opportunity to confront our fears, discover there's nothing to fear, step through them in love, and let them go. Old ways of seeing, believing, and doing pass away and space opens for ways of fearless seeing, understanding and doing. We step into our autonomy. It's there for each of us.

Jesus said it this way,

If you are searching, you must not stop until you find.
When you find ... you will become troubled.
Your confusion will give way to wonder.
In wonder you will reign over all things.
Your sovereignty will be your rest.

— *The Gospel of Thomas*

The apocalypse is not *the end time*. It's a *beginning again time*. As more and more of us move through apotheosis, human consciousness is transformed and the veil between heaven and earth disappears.

Through my dreams and paintings, I've visited places on the Earth a thousand years from now. Our planet is renewed, healthy and brimming with life. It's an amazingly beautiful place. Many fewer humans inhabit the Earth. Men and women stand side-by-side as creators and caretakers. We live in harmony with each other, the planet and all her creatures.

That is good news—the new good news.

Genesis

DAD BARGED INTO my room.

He didn't knock or anything. He said he wanted to talk.

Jeepers, I thought. It's *the talk.*

I'd been worrying about *the talk.* I'd just turned 11. My friend Jimmy got *the talk* when he was 11. He said it was about putting your wiener in a girl and getting a baby out.

"Gross," I said.

Jimmy said *the talk* made his hands sweaty.

My hands were sweaty, too.

"Relax," Dad said. "I didn't come in here to talk about sex, boy. Avoiding the subject of sex is a Johnson family tradition."

He laughed like he'd told a joke.

"Came in here to talk about life, boy—your life—not because you need it, but because your mother is on me to do it and I'm not gonna hear the end of it till I do. So listen up."

"Yes sir," I said.

"Don't worry about any of this now. Have some fun. It's the only fun you're gonna have in your life. Don't tell your mother I said that."

"Yes sir," I said.

"We gotta be realistic about where you're headed, boy. You're no Babe Ruth. You can't sing a lick and your piano teacher says we're wasting our money. You haven't got a God-given talent that'll save you from a normal life and that's okay. Most of us do life the regular way. There's no shame in it."

"Yes, sir," I said.

"Soon you'll be going to high school. You're gonna have to buckle down. You're gonna get A's on your report card, play football, and get elected president of something so you can get into a decent college. Got that?"

"Yes, sir," I said.

"In college, you'll study some but mostly try to get laid. It won't happen much, but you'll spend most of your time trying anyway. Then you'll fall in love with some girl and she'll dump you and break your heart. Happens to all of us. Don't let it get you down. You'll graduate with a degree in English or Philosophy or who-knows-what. It won't be worth much, but you'll need it to get into graduate school. That's where you'll learn something useful, like law or business."

"Yes sir, but I want to be a doctor like you."

"The government's taking over medicine, son. You don't want to work for the government, do you?" He shook his head. He didn't seem to think working for the government was a good idea.

"No sir," I said.

"Good," he said. "Next you'll find yourself a nice girl from a good family. You'll have to be pleasant for a year or so before she'll marry you. After you're married, you'll get laid all the time and have three kids." (He explained why three was the right number, but I've forgotten that part.)

"You'll move into a big house on a hill in a good neighborhood and get yourself a fancy car—an Oldsmobile like mine. You'll work like hell, raise your children, send them off into the world, retire, and fiddle around waiting for grandchildren. If you're lucky, you'll get to spoil them for a few years before you die."

Dad checked his watch and shook his head.

"Got that?"

"Yes, sir. Is that it?"

"It's the American Dream, son. Any questions?"

"What does *get laid* mean?"

"We'll tackle that another time," he said. "Gotta run."

And he ran.

I'm a go-getter if there ever was one. I couldn't wait till high school. I started living like Dad said. I was going to make him proud.

I respected my elders and obeyed my teachers.

I won a golf tournament when I was 12 and got a silver-plated cereal bowl with my name engraved in the bottom of it.

"Nice job," Dad said.

I was president of my junior high class.

I learned to waltz at The Fort Nightly School of Dance and got some manners. I also learned how to write a girl's name on a dance card. That's certainly been useful.

I went on to high school—an all-boys school in my hometown of Nashville, Tennessee.

I studied and got good grades.

I dated some pretty girls and was a gentleman most of the time.

I played football. I didn't much care for it. But I played anyway so I could put it on my college applications.

"One more thing," Dad said. "It's best to keep your thing in your pants. It may be little but it can get you into a heap of trouble."

"It's not little," I said.

At 18, I finagled my way into college, studied some and spent a lot of time trying to get laid. It didn't happen much, but I tried all the time anyway.

"I knew you weren't gonna keep your thing in your pants," Dad said. "But it was something I had to say."

I fell in love with a girl. I was head-over-heels for her. I wanted to get laid with her, but she said no. She said she wasn't getting laid until she got married. So I said I'd marry her.

"No thanks," she said.

She broke my heart. It got me down—way down.

"I told you not to let it get you down," Dad said.

Soon thereafter, I graduated from college with a degree in English, found out it wasn't going to pay for my American Dream, and went on to graduate school.

While there, I met a nice girl from a good family. I was pleasant enough I guess, because after a year or so she said she'd marry me. Her name was Neal.

"You married over your head," she said. "Don't forget to tell 'em that part."

After we married, I got laid a lot and fathered three beautiful daughters.

"You're making it sound like you did the work," she said. "You didn't do all that much and it wasn't what I'd call work."

While Neal raised the girls, I played lawyer for a while and then businessman. Along the way, we accumulated stuff—lots of stuff. I drove around in fancy cars—never an Oldsmobile, but fancy enough. We lived in some big houses. The last one was on a hill in a good neighborhood in Seattle. We had a spectacular lake view.

Finally got the big house on a hill, I thought. *I'm summiting the American Dream.*

To pay our debt to society, Neal and I supported a handful of charities and ate Chicken Kiev at fancy charity balls.

"I never cared for Chicken Kiev," she said.

Our daughters grew up and moved on. They took their cars with them.

I sold my business interests, put some money in the bank, and retired earlier than I'd expected.

I had everything I'd ever wanted.

I'd done everything Dad told me to do, except the Oldsmobile.

I'd lived my life on the American Dream checklist and checked all the boxes except the last two: SPOIL GRANDCHILDREN and DIE.

I thought I'd be happy when I was done with the list.

I told myself I *should* be happy.

But I wasn't happy.

Bought the Farm

"WHY ARE YOU moping?" Neal wanted to know. "You have everything you've ever wanted."

"Maybe that's the problem. I have everything I want. I should be happy but I'm not. Wanting is what keeps me going and there's nothing more I want. The only thing I care about is you and the girls and a few friends. The stuff we have isn't making me happy and I hate taking care of it. Seems all I do is wash stuff and wax stuff and change the oil in stuff and paint stuff and sweep stuff and mow stuff and prune stuff and …"

"Well, maybe we should get rid of some stuff. Simplify our lives. We can ditch this life and get a new one," Neal said. "Leave the American Dream behind. Find a new dream."

"Really? What'll we do?"

"I want to be an Earth mother," she said. "I want to get my hands dirty, walk around barefoot, tie my hair up in colorful scarves and adorn myself with turquoise necklaces to highlight my liquid blue eyes."

"Sounds good," I said.

So we went off script. Instead of rambling around in our big house waiting for grandchildren and the grim reaper, we sold the house, ditched a lot of stuff, packed up the little we kept, and moved to the country where we planned to build a small wood-framed farmhouse with a tin roof, get ourselves a couple of straw hats, grow zucchini squash, and sit on a shady porch with a couple of sleepy farm dogs.

We had a new dream and went after it hammer and tong. We were go-getters again.

We bought land—too much of it—way out on the prairie. A river ran through it. We built a farmhouse with a shady front porch and fenced a couple of acres for the dogs. From our rockers on the porch, we had a spectacular view of snow-capped mountains. The zucchini grew like weeds and the weeds outpaced the zucchini.

"Nice," I said.

"We need a barn," Neal said.

"A what?"

"For our tractor and other farm stuff. We've got a lot of land, honey. We're going to need stuff to take care of the land."

"Jeepers," I said. "I guess…"

"And we need a cottage for the kids and another bedroom in the house and maybe we should go ahead and finish the attic—put in bunk beds and a bathroom and…"

"For what?" I asked.

"For the grandchildren. We can't live out here in the hinterlands and forget about our kids and the grandchildren."

"But we don't have any grandchildren."

"We will. Several of them. And we'll need a pony for them to ride, and some goats to pet, and I'd like to have a horse—maybe a couple of horses in case a friend wants to ride with me—and you'll need a horse, and we'll need a horse trailer and a truck to pull the trailer. And I want to raise chickens so we'll need a chicken coop."

In no time, we accumulated more stuff than we had before we decided to downsize and simplify our lives.

We commenced changing the oil in stuff and painting stuff and weeding stuff and mowing stuff and washing stuff and…well…I guess you get the picture. We hired Ray to help us take care of our stuff.

"This is a lot of stuff," I said.

"Well, we can't live on this farm without it," Neal said.

"But…"

"Let's not have any of your *buts*, honey. If you don't like tending the farm, Ray and I will do it. I think you're too prissy for farming anyway."

"I'm *not* prissy," I said.

"Sure you are, honey. You won't wear your straw hat because you're afraid of getting it dirty."

"So what'll I do?"

"Don't know. Just do something you *love* to do, not something you think you *should* do. You've done that all your life. Do something your heart loves. Listen to your heart."

"My heart's not saying anything."

"Goodness, honey. Give it some time."

Write Something

A FEW DAYS later, Neal had an idea, "Honey, I know what you should do."

"*Should* do? I thought I was looking for something my heart loves."

"Well, think of me as your heart's messenger. You should write a book. You're too prissy for farming and you've always wanted to write and writers are prissy. At least most of 'em are."

"Hmm…" I said.

Here's where I tell you about one of the books I wrote. It's a book about my fascinating childhood. A big-deal New York publisher published it. It was in stores all over the place. I went on a book tour. I was on radio and TV. Life was full of hope. I got a new career, 30 days of fame, and something short of big bucks for my effort.

Unfortunately, the book never made the bestseller list—not even close. My writing career foundered and dashed itself on the rocks as quickly as it arrived.

I returned from the book tour expecting a welcome-home celebration.

"Sorry honey, I didn't have time to throw a party," Neal said. She tucked a wisp of blonde hair behind her ear, but it fell back in her face. "This farm work is eating me up. Plus you hate parties. Plus you're on a diet. So I didn't bake a cake or anything. But I got you this nice bottle of wine. Welcome home! And now that's done, so come help me spread manure on the river pasture. The horse shit is piling up on us."

"Thanks for the wine," I said.

After we spread manure, Neal washed her hands and went into the kitchen to do some baking. I washed my hands, went through the kitchen to the porch and sat down in my chair.

Yoda came and sat beside me. Yoda's my dog—a low-slung Corgi with a limited vocabulary, extra-long ears, steady brown eyes, a prominent nose and a ground-sweeping belly. He's a lot like me. Laying about the porch is his favorite thing to do.

"Are you glad I'm home?" I asked.

"Arooooooo," Yoda said. (That's as close as he gets to a bark.)

"Thank you. I'm 60, you know. Never dreamed I'd get this far. But here I am. I've had a good life. I've done everything I ever wanted to do plus a few extras. I've checked off everything on my life list except grandchildren and the grand finale."

"Arooooooo," Yoda said.

"I have no earthly idea what to do next."

"You'll figure it out," Neal yelled from the kitchen. "Like you did with your book."

"That book didn't do much."

"Sure it did. It kept your hands out of the devil's workshop for a couple of years. That was an accomplishment."

"Arooooooo," Yoda said. He nodded his head and rolled over on his back so I could scratch his belly.

The porch fan turned slowly overhead. A gaggle of geese rose from the river and settled on the spring-fed pond beyond the root cellar. The faint scent of fresh-baked bread wafted through the screen door behind me.

"Thank goodness my health's good and my mind's sound."

"Not *that* sound," Neal quipped. "You've got a terrible memory and it's getting worse, honey. You don't notice it, but everybody else does. I've been meaning to talk to you about it. We need to work on that."

"I've come to the end of my life's path and I don't know which way to turn."

"It's not the end of your path. It's just the end of the part you can see. Same thing happened before you wrote your book. Listen to your heart. What you'll do next is in there somewhere."

The geese startled and rose into the sky again, chased by a couple of juvenile coyotes. They circled several times and dropped back onto the river.

"Wonder how many years I have left?"

"Don't know," Neal said.

The yeasty scent of baking bread wafted onto the porch again.

"C'mon Yoda, let's do a little research and check on the bread."

"Arooooooo," Yoda said, trundling into the house behind me.

About that time Neal pulled a crusty, whole-grain loaf from the oven—a specialty loaded with fiber, full of walnuts, pumpkin seeds and prunes. I reached for the bread knife.

"Leave it," Neal said, wagging a finger at me. "It has to cool."

"But..."

"None of your *buts*, honey. I'll slice the bread when it's ready and not before."

Sitting at the kitchen table with a mug of coffee and my computer, I waited for the bread to cool and searched the worldwide web for life-expectancy data. It didn't look good. I sorted the data over and over, trying to tease out better news, but sorting didn't help.

"What's it say?" Neal wanted to know.

"It says I have 20 years to go more or less—maybe way less. And even if I get 20 years, I'd be unwise to count on 20 years of perfect health. Some of those years I'll probably be bedridden or wandering the land of bunnies."

"Twenty years is a long time," she said.

"Not *that* long. The last 20 went by fast—*really* fast."

"Something good's gonna happen. You just wait and see. Pray about it. Ask God for guidance. He'll help you if you ask real nice."

"Hard to imagine. I'm not much of a church-goer."

"He'll take you back. God's not one to hold a grudge. He'll be grateful you've finally come around."

"Well, if I were God I'd be pissed."

"That's one of the many reasons you're not God, honey."

"Arooooooo," Yoda said.

"God'll help you. Let him do his thing. Just tell him you're up for whatever comes and let him have the wheel. You're always trying to *do* something. Let go. Go with the flow. See what happens."

"But I don't know how to do that," I said.

"Lordy," Neal said, shaking her head.

A few nights later, I lay in bed in the dark, head propped up on several pillows, eyes closed, stewing about my life. What was it all about? Why couldn't I find the silver lining? Why wasn't I happy?

Then *BANG!* It was an explosion of some sort. Brilliant white light flashed in front of me somewhere. My eyes were closed so I didn't see anything—just the brilliant light behind my eyelids and the BANG.

"What was that?" Neal startled. "Are you okay?"

"I think so. I heard a loud bang and a light flashed somewhere. I had my eyes closed…"

"Yikes, honey! It was a ball of lightning. Like lightning but a ball… like a ball of swirling lightning. It came through the window. I saw it coming out of the sky across the field. It came through the window and hit you in the head. Are you okay?"

"I'm fine. I didn't feel anything. Maybe a little pressure on my forehead…"

"It hit you in the head, honey. Seriously, I'd be dead if that'd hit me in the head."

"I'm okay," I said. "I feel fine. Wonder what it was?"

"I don't know. That was wild!"

"Let's go back to sleep," I said. "It must have been a dream."

"That was no dream, honey. I saw it, whatever it was. And the bang. Maybe it was some sort of sign or something."

"Maybe so," I said. "Maybe so…"

Uncharted Waters

SHORTLY THEREAFTER, I found myself planning a trip home—to Nashville, Tennessee where this wondrous life began.

"Good idea," Neal said. "Get away for a while. See your mom. Maybe going home will lighten you up."

I'm here on this Earth because my mother—everybody called her Coco—wanted a baby girl. Had she gotten that little girl instead of me, I might never have been. I think about that sometimes—how iffy my life has been. It's a sobering thought. And that's not all, had Coco gotten her little girl, some number of my four younger brothers wouldn't be here either. It's entirely possible that none of us would be here.

My brother Randy arrived eighteen months after me.

Coco lay on the delivery room table, bare feet in cold metal stirrups, worn out after 17 hours of labor, but still her normally cheerful self.

"It's another boy," the doctor said.

"What?" Coco blurted. "You've got to be kidding, Doc. Nine months plus seventeen hours of hell and you're telling me I've got another boy?"

"Kinda looks that way," he said.

Coco dabbed the sweat from her brow with a wet washcloth, swirled a few ice chips around on her parched tongue, and gave in to exhaustion. Tears welled up in the corners of her eyes.

"Oh well…maybe next time," she said, trying but mostly failing to hold back the tears. "My odds gotta be improving. Surely they're improving."

Then Larry came along.

Home from the hospital, Coco took to pacing back and forth between the crib room and the kitchen with a baby under each arm, muttering, "Boys, I'm wandering around under a dark cloud—a very dark cloud."

Then came Tommy.

"Dear God!" Coco pleaded, looking up at the dining-room chandelier. "I know you're punishing me for something. Maybe you're still mad about that late-night walk with Jimmy Lee after the prom. I don't know. But I've wracked my brain and can't come up with anything else. I've already said I'm sorry and I meant it."

Then along came Gary.

"Oh my," the doctor said. "It's another boy."

"Lord, take me," Coco said, covering her head with her arms. "How can that be?" she whimpered.

The doctor stood quietly at the foot of the delivery table while Coco came to grips with the harsh reality of a life she'd never imagined.

"Could this be my life? Five boys and not even one little girl?"

The doctor placed a rubber-gloved hand gently on Coco's foot.

"It's gonna be alright," he said.

"Well, I reckon we're gonna see about that, aren't we?" Coco said dejectedly. "Doc, this is the end of the line for me. I'm not having another go. So go on. While you're down there, tie those boy-happy tubes in a double knot. I'm throwing in the towel."

→—⊚ ⊚—←

Coco raised all five of us boys—mostly by herself.

Dad was a doctor. He went to the hospital every day and brought home money. That was a good thing as far as it went, but he wasn't much help around the house.

"I'm a saint," Coco said, sitting at her kitchen table sipping a diet orange soda. She'd just celebrated her 87ᵗʰ birthday. "That's all there is to it. I'm tootin' my own horn, I know. But if I don't blow it, nobody else will."

Coco's right, of course. If there's any justice in heaven, she'll be canonized a saint when she dies.

As we talked, Coco shifted uncomfortably in her chair. She'd grown frail and tired but her mind was sharp and she'd hung onto her sense of humor.

"All you have to do is die," I told her. "You raised five boys to manhood—not one axe murderer in the bunch. And you've lived a virtuous life except for your late-night walk in the garden with Jimmy Lee."

"How'd you hear about that?" she yipped.

"You told me yourself, years ago."

"Well, you leave Jimmy Lee out of this, young man," Coco barked. Her eyes flashed. "That's none of your darn business. And anyway, it was just one measly little slip…"

"You've performed numerous miracles with Mercurochrome," I went on, trying to get us past Jimmy Lee.

"And Ipecac," Coco added. "Don't forget the Ipecac. I saved a lot of lives with vomiting."

"Yes ma'am, you did. And if you can perform miracles here on earth, surely you can orchestrate a few from heaven. When you do, you'll have met all the sainthood requirements."

"Good thing I joined the Catholic Church," she said. "Maybe I should start going again. You think us holier-than-thou Catholics have a lock on sainthood like they say? Doesn't seem right, does it?"

"No, but I read somewhere you get your own feast day if you become a saint. The Feast of Saint Coco, they'll call it."

"Really?" Coco tapped her cheek with an index finger and thought for a bit, warming to the idea. "My very own feast day. Think of that. Has a nice ring to it, doesn't it?"

"Yes, it does."

"Meatloaf," Coco said thoughtfully. "If I'm going to have my own feast day, folks should serve my meatloaf, don't you think? And my macaroni-and-cheese and my three-bean salad and my turnip greens, of course. And my pickled shrimp for an appetizer. Everybody loves my pickled shrimp. And maybe my lemon squares for dessert. And...will they be serving alcohol?"

"Don't know."

"Well, if they're serving alcohol, you'll tell 'em about my whiskey sours, won't you?"

"Yes, ma'am," I said.

"Good, 'cause folks love my whiskey sours."

She paused to adjust the pillow in her chair and went on, "Speaking of feasts, what are we having for dinner?"

Coco had pretty much given up her car keys, so my visit was an opportunity to *order out.*

"Whatever you want," I said.

"The Colonel's chicken livers. I've been thinking about 'em since I heard you were coming. And a side of slaw. And those biscuits. And mashed potatoes. And gravy."

"You know that stuff's not good for you..." I started.

"And none of your preaching. I'll have a side order of silence. There's not a darn thing the Colonel can do to this body that hasn't already been done."

"Fair point," I said.

Over the next few days, I ate carry-out with Coco—Southern, Chinese, Mexican, and Thai. I drank coffee with friends. I walked a lot. I even drove around the old neighborhood, reviving childhood memories. It was a nice trip as far as it went.

On my last night in Nashville, I ate an early dinner with Coco (more chicken livers), said goodbye several times (Coco had a lot to say), finally got out the door, and went back to my hotel room. I sat on the edge of the bed and flipped through TV channels. Even though I'd mostly enjoyed the visit, I felt empty again. My trip hadn't shed light on anything but new sources of indigestion. I went through the motions of brushing my teeth, downed a handful of Tums, turned off the lights, and went to bed. As I lay on my back in the pitch-black dark, I noticed the tiny green light on the smoke detector above my head and said out loud: *There's got to be more than this.*

⊷⟫ ⟪⊶

Back at the farm after a long day of flying, Neal and I sat in front of the fire drinking a glass of wine. Yoda lay beside my chair nudging my hand into action.

"So?" Neal started.

"So?"

"So how's Coco and who'd you see and what did you do and what did you learn about the next chapter in your life. When you get back from a trip, honey, you're supposed to sit with your beautiful wife in front of a warm fire, pet your dog, and talk."

"Right," I said.

We talked about Coco and her failing health—the challenges she faced every day just getting through the day. We talked about old friends and how Nashville's changed. Then I told her about the emptiness and saying there had to be more.

Neal's eyes suddenly widened like she'd seen a ghost.

"Lord, honey," she said. "You've tipped your apple cart in the middle of the street. There's no getting the apples back now."

"What?" I said.

"Things are changing for you."

"How do you know..." I started.

"Trust me," she said softly, staring into the fire.

I woke early the next morning and, before brushing my teeth, I cleaned out my closet. In no time at all, plastic trash bags full of old clothes littered the hallway.

Clearing out my closet felt good, so I cleaned out the file cabinet in my study. Then I cleaned out my car—even the glove compartment. I stacked the oil change receipts in chronological order. Then I went out to the barn and cleaned out a room full of boxes we'd been carting around with us for a lifetime. Then I cleaned more stuff out of my closet. I took it all to Goodwill.

"What's with all the cleaning?" Neal asked.

"Don't know. Can't help it."

"You're getting pretty anal, honey. And you're losing weight. Have you noticed that? It's like you're training for something. Are you training for something?"

"Don't think so."

"Well you're clearing the decks for something."

"What do you think it is?" I asked.

"Don't know," Neal said. "Guess we'll have to wait and see. God's getting you ready for something."

Over the next few months, I lost more weight, cleared out more stuff, and started doing all kinds of spiritual things.

I read about Jesus and the Buddha and desert mystics.

I went on a meditation retreat in California. (Where else?)

I consulted a psychic. Through him, I talked to my dad even though he was dead. Dad didn't have much to say. He mostly wished I drove an Oldsmobile.

About that time, a level-headed friend told me he'd visited a Brazilian healer named John of God and had an amazing spiritual experience. I'd never heard of him, but I did a little research and discovered millions of people had visited John of God. Some saw him as the most powerful spiritual healer since Jesus. One of the websites I found said my healing—whatever that was—would start as soon as I signed up to go to Brazil. I didn't have to wait till I got there.

I was skeptical. *A faith healer? Really? C'mon people, get a grip…*

At the time, I had no illnesses to speak of. Sure, I got my annual cold and had an occasional run-in with indigestion. But that's about it. As far as I knew, I didn't need to be healed.

"You don't need a reason to go," Neal said. "If your heart's telling you to go, go. I think it'll be good for you. You're chomping at the bit to get out of here. Go see what happens."

So I signed up with a tour group and bought plane tickets. I'd be leaving for Brazil in a couple of months.

Shortly after I signed up, I woke in the middle of a moonless winter night and heard a voice. It was a female voice. It said, "Time to go, child."

"What?" I said aloud. "Who are you? Go where?"

"God got da pen, child."

"What?" I blurted, turning on the bedside lamp.

"What?" Neal mumbled, burrowing under her heavy patchwork quilt.

"I don't know. I heard a voice. A woman was here talking to me."

"What'd she say?"

"She said it was time to go."

"Go where?"

"I don't know. She said *God got da pen.* Sounded like an old black woman."

"An angel," Neal said. "Go back to sleep, honey. She'll be back when you need her. She'll let you know when you need to know."

"And how would you know that?"

"I'm a woman. I know these things. Now turn off the light and go back to sleep."

Over the next several weeks , the voice—quiet, loving and persistent—came and went, always saying the same thing. *Time to go, child. God got da pen.*

I developed a vague sense I was going to Nashville to spend more time with Coco and work on a project of some sort.

"Where's that coming from?" Neal wanted to know.

"I have no idea," I said. "I just feel it. I can't explain it."

Then came the day I knew I was leaving.

"Could that be right?" I asked myself.

"Yes, child," the voice said.

"Really?" I said. "You've got to be kidding. Leave the farm and my family and friends and Yoda?"

"Time to go, child," the voice said. "God got da pen."

Suddenly I had clarity. I was moving back to Nashville.

I talked to Neal about it.

She nodded and said, "You're not the only one hearing voices, honey. I heard one this morning down by the river. It was God."

"Really?"

"He said I was to let you go. He said you have things to do."

She looked at me with her liquid blue eyes. Tears welled up in them. I held her—just held her—wondering where our lives were taking us. Whatever illusions we had about controlling our lives were shattering.

"We're going with the flow," Neal said.

"You've always said we should do that."

"Right," she said. "And it's scaring me...really scaring me."

In that moment, without so much as a howdy-do, my life took a hard-right turn, went off road, and flipped over in the Cottonwoods where, unbeknownst to me, my spiritual path was waiting in dense underbrush.

Spiritual Healing

DAYS LATER I boarded a plane for Brazil. I flew all night and met my tour group in Brasilia where we loaded into vans for the ride to the village of Abadiania.

I sat with a young woman named Jenkins and her mother and sister. Among other things, I learned that Jenkins lived in Nashville and was traveling to Brazil seeking help for breast cancer. I felt a strange connection with her—like I somehow knew her. Her mom and sister were making the trip to support her and there were others from Nashville on the van—a wonderful group. Before the trip ended, they'd be my new Nashville friends.

A few of our fellow travelers had visible physical ailments. Mary suffered from advancing blindness. Jay and Wendy lived with severe, chronic pain from long-ago car accidents. Jay was so crippled that, even after a dizzying series of head and spinal surgeries, he wore neck and back braces around the clock and hobbled his way through life. He had an irrepressible spirit, but said his ailments were getting worse, not better. He was skeptical of spiritual healers but out of options and willing to try most anything. This trip was his last best chance to get some relief.

The rest of our group suffered unseen illnesses—cancers, heart problems, neurological diseases and other disorders. We were, mostly, a very sick bunch.

"What brought you here?" Wendy asked.

"I don't know," I said. "Curiosity, I guess."

I felt guilty for being healthy.

-»-»=◎ ◎=◄-◄-

The Casa of Joao de Deus sits on a hillside high above a lush jungle valley. A post-and-beam pavilion perches precariously on the edge of a red-clay cliff overlooking the valley. It's adorned with a wooden triangle nailed to one of the posts. On the sides of the triangle are the words— *Amor, Fe* and *Caridad*.

Shortly after we arrived in Abadiania, I stood at the pavilion's wood railing and listened to unfamiliar jungle noises while emerald-green parrots slipped in and out of the forest canopy. The air was warm. A billow of dark clouds hung ominously above the hills on the horizon.

Pilgrims like me lined the pavilion's benches. Most sat with their eyes closed, their lips offering quiet prayers, their hands working strands of beads. Some read their Bibles. An old French woman fingered the yellowed pages of a second-hand romance novel. The word *Inferno* was visible on its spine. A family of dark-eyed Brazilians napped on the floor next to her. A young couple leaned on the railing next to me whispering in Dutch, looking through a guidebook.

Manicured gardens full of wild orchids, bougainvillea, and saintly statues surrounded us. The whitewashed buildings of the Casa stood on the hill behind us in a watercolor sky. It was a holy place. It was a place for praying if I'd ever seen one. So, I screwed up my courage and prayed for the first time in a very long time.

Dear God,

If you're listening…

I hope you're listening.

You said you'd listen even if I am a sinner—which I undoubtedly am. So here goes.

I hereby and henceforth take my hands off the wheel. I'm all yours.

I stopped to admire the *hereby and henceforth*. Adding some legalese made the whole thing seem more formal and binding. I continued...

You're right. I've said those very words before. I don't blame you for being skeptical. I would be too. But I'm serious this time. I really mean it.

May I learn to move through the rest of my blessed life like a feather on your breath.

And you're right about that too. That's not my line. Somebody else said it. I don't remember who said it, but it seems appropriate here.

So, just to be clear, I'll say it again.

May I be like a feather on the breath of God.

Suddenly—out of nowhere—a gale-force wind whipped us prayerful pilgrims like the spinning soapy slappers in a drive-thru car wash. An unripe mango crashed on the pavilion deck next to the old French woman. She sprang from her crouch and bolted like a cheetah.

Serves her right for reading that trash, I thought.

(Yes, it was an unkind thought. I have those sometimes.)

The rest of us were right behind her.

I covered my head with both arms and sprinted uphill toward the nearest building. Biblical tracts, crumpled pieces of paper, orchid blossoms, palm fronds, paper cups, plastic zip-lock bags, and the rest of God's creation littered the air as we fled.

All hell broke loose.

The Brazilian family ducked into a tiny shed ahead of me. I ducked in behind them. We stood there drenched and shivering—staring at one another.

"Sorry. My bad," I said.

The Brazilian father shrugged.

A small gray feather blew in through the open door. It stuck to a raindrop on my nose.

The morning following the *feather incident* was hot, still and muggy. Hundreds of pilgrims walked silently toward the Casa. They were dressed head-to-toe in white. I'd never seen so many people slumped in wheel chairs and struggling on crutches.

When I arrived at the Casa, I joined the line to see John of God. As I followed the line into the Casa sanctuary, I saw people sitting silently in church pews on either side of the center aisle, heads bowed, eyes closed.

John of God sat in a chair welcoming each of us in the line as we approached him. While I waited for my blessing, I watched people in front of me drop their crutches or rise from their wheelchairs. They walked out of the sanctuary unaided.

"Unbelievable," I said under my breath.

John of God, a heavy-set elderly gentleman with thinning black hair, a square jaw and penetrating eyes, is Brazilian and speaks Portuguese. An interpreter introduced me. John of God looked at me in an odd, quizzical way—studying me like he knew me but couldn't place me. I had the sudden, but inexplicable, feeling I'd be doing healing work myself one day.

When he spoke, he invited me to sit in the sanctuary and pray for those coming to the Casa. As I sat, I thought about the strangeness of the encounter. *No,* I thought. *That can't be true. Not me. I'm no healer.*

For the next two weeks, I occupied a seat beneath an old-time oscillating fan in the Casa's sanctuary as thousands paraded down the aisle for healing. When I wasn't praying, I dozed to escape boredom and all the unanswerable questions. When I wasn't napping, I studied the folks around me. Without opening my eyes, I noticed the lady in front of me who snorted loudly and woke herself every few minutes only to fall back asleep, snort again and wake herself. I found I could predict the next snort. The elderly couple to my left scuffled off and on over the right to control a handheld paper fan. I rooted for the husband who sat next to me, fanned himself vigorously, and created a bit of additional breeze for both of us. In hot, humid Abadiania any breeze was a welcome breeze. The lady behind me sometimes rested her head on the back of my pew, pushing me to lean forward in my seat so she could sleep more comfortably.

Only once did I have anything approaching a spiritual experience. During a fitful daydream, I saw myself standing on a high hill looking out over a valley. A brown fabric stretched as far as I could see across the valley floor and rippled like a giant American flag during halftime at the Super Bowl. My perception shifted and I realized it wasn't a flag or fabric. It was thousands upon thousands of damaged human beings on crutches and in wheelchairs—all moving toward something unseen. My perception shifted again and I noticed these broken people were not just in the valley below me but surrounding me.

What's that about? I wondered, as a tear rolled down my cheek.

Walking from the Casa back to my hotel, I heard someone calling my name. I turned around. Jay was running—not hobbling—toward me. He was screaming, "I'm well! No pain! No braces! Steve, I'm well! I'm well! It's a miracle!"

And it was.

Soul Food

A FEW DAYS after I returned to the farm, I hugged Neal goodbye. She opened the farm gate for me and I drove away.

I had my car and three boxes of stuff that fit neatly in the trunk. I pointed the nose of the car toward Nashville.

My drive covered 2000 miles. I rarely listen to the radio, so I drove in silence—mostly feeling lonely, but sometimes oddly light and free.

During one pitifully lonely stretch—somewhere in the middle of an endless Nebraska cornfield—I thought, *What the hell am I doing? I've just walked away from a perfect life—a wonderful wife, a beautiful farm, old friends, and a very comfortable existence. It was everything I ever wanted. I was living my dream. What the hell have I done?*

"You rememberin', child."

It was the voice.

"You're back," I said, "Really? Well about damn time. You're the one who got me into this mess—all that *go child* crap. Now look at the fix I'm in. I've just thrown away my life. You know that? Do you understand what I'm saying? I've just thrown away a perfect life—the life I dreamed of."

The voice and I'd never had a conversation. All she'd ever said was *God got da pen* and *go child* and stuff like that. There was no back-and-forth. But now I was alone and lonely. I didn't have anybody to talk to. Nobody could hear me.

I'm certifiably crazy, I thought. *I'm hearing voices. Maybe I'm going nuts. Hell, maybe I'm already nuts and just don't know it.*

I needed to vent, so I went on...

"Just for the record, this may be the stupidest thing I've ever done. Seriously. The stupidest."

Suddenly Art Carney, the movie star, was sitting next to me in the passenger seat with a cat in his lap and just as suddenly he was gone.

"What was that?" I blurted. "Art Carney. He was here in my car. I am nuts!"

"Eye on da road," the voice said.

Nearly 40 years ago, Neal and I went to see *Harry and Tonto*—the movie. I remember it vividly mostly because it stirred deep emotions in me. At the end of the show, I blubbered like a baby. I sat in the emptying theater with Neal, crying my eyes out. I couldn't remember the last time I'd cried.

"What's that about?" Neal wanted to know, "I've never seen a tear out of you."

"I don't know," I said. "That movie got to me. I don't know why."

We were the last to leave the theater and we drove home in silence.

"What you thinkin'?" the voice asked.

"I'm remembering a movie," I said. "*Harry and Tonto*. A long time ago. It was about an old guy named Harry. Art Carney was Harry. I think he won an Academy Award or something. I haven't thought about that movie in years. I remember it got to me for some reason—made me cry. I don't know why. I never figured it out."

"And?" the voice prompted.

"Harry was retired and living in New York. He was bored—just going through the motions, waiting to die. Then the city condemned his apartment building. It was a big mess. He tried to hang on, but the city threw him out. He had to move. All he had was his cat and a suitcase. He went to live with his son somewhere in the New York suburbs. Brooklyn maybe. He hated it there.

"So, one day Harry left—picked up his suitcase and his cat and took off. He bought an old car at a used car lot and headed west. Along the way, he had all kinds of adventures—just blowing in the wind—and ended up in California with his beater car and his cat and his suitcase. It all worked out."

"Sound like anybody you know, child?"

"I guess..."

"Why dat movie get you, child?"

"I don't know," I said. "I can't explain it. I don't know what that was about."

"I thinkin' you do," said the voice.

"I don't..."

I caught myself. I drove in the silence for a long while. I don't know how long. I drove—thinking about the movie. Then I said...

"Because I knew this day was coming."

There was silence.

No voice.

Just silence.

And then...

I lost it. I wept. The tears came from deep in me somewhere. What I'd said was true. Way back then something in me knew this time was coming in my life. I'd be making my own cross-country trip one of these days.

"I get it," I said. "I'm driving cross-country with three boxes of stuff. I'm living the movie—my version of the movie."

"And what you feelin', child?"

"Lonely but kind of free. It's hard to describe. It's like I'm finally doing this thing I have to do—like my soul can breathe."

"And dat be a start."

"Maybe..."

"God got da pen, child. He writin'. You doin' the livin'. Dis what your soul been wantin'."

I let her words sink in.

"I have no idea where I'm going," I said. "What I'm doing..."

"No need to know," the voice said. "You got me."

"Who are you?"

"We gonna talk 'bout dat," the voice said. "We got a heap o' work to do..."

Sarah

WHEN I FIRST heard the voice saying *God got da pen* and *time to go*, Neal said it was an angel talking to me.

I didn't believe her. I wasn't into angels—certainly not ones who talked to me.

I figured the voice was something I made up—one of the infinite number of voices in my head spinning stories like they always do, offering up the paranoid, delusional stuff that makes me miserable. Why I put up with that mess is beyond me.

But this voice was different. It was clear and distinct. It was female and spoke in the dialect of an old southern black woman. Loving and comfortable, it sounded familiar.

I grew up under the supervision of an old black woman. Her name was Sarah. She lived on a farm outside Jackson, Tennessee, with my aunt and uncle. I took up residence at the farm during the summer months of my childhood and Sarah was, for all practical purposes, my summer mother.

She hovered over my brothers and me all day long. She stripped us *nekkid* at the well pump and scrubbed us head to toe before we were allowed back in the house after a day of rolling around in barnyard muck. She baited our hooks when we went down to the pond. She fed us fried perch and mashed potatoes and butter beans for dinner. She talked to Jesus all day long and found the devil in the most unlikely places. She was pure magic.

"Sarah?" I said.

"Yes, child," she said. "Now you gettin' it."

"Jeepers," I said. "It's you! Really? But you're dead. You died... I don't even know..."

"Nineteen and seventy-two," she said.

"Forty years ago," I said. "I can't see you but I can hear you."

"You'll see, child," she said. "You will..."

A few weeks later, I glimpsed her briefly.

"That you, Sarah?"

"Yes, child. You seein' me, ain't you? Good."

"Amazing."

Her image disappeared, but her voice remained.

"You're a ghost and you look different. Not like I remember. I remember you...well...thinner....you've put on weight."

"Lots of folks sayin' that," she chuckled.

"You're really back?"

"Yes, child. I's back. Ol' Sarah now yo' helper –yo' muse."

"Muse?"

"Yes, child."

"I have a muse who murders the English language?"

"That what spell-check for, child."

"I saw muses in a picture once—in my Latin book in high school—three of them and all were leggy blondes with perky breasts wearing see-through negligees. What happened to my leggy blondes?"

"I's what you got, child. Beggars don't get no choosin'. We be jus' fine without no leggy blondes."

Sarah knots her gray-specked hair into a frizzy ball on the back of her head and covers it with a red bandana. Plump cheeks scrunch her brown eyes into a squint. She totes a heavy cast-iron skillet in her meaty hands, looking like she might use it for something other than frying cornbread.

"You can be hard-headed," she says.

Sarah wears a blue work dress under her white apron. Her apron is torn at the sash, mended with a safety pin, and splattered with a lot of who-knows-what across her ample bosom.

"Nobody never called Sarah's old bosoms *perky*," she says.

Sarah is one of my companions. I don't see her anymore, but I hear her. She seems to hover above my right ear.

Sometimes I think I'm making the whole thing up.

"Nuh-uh, child, you ain't making nothin' up. I's right here takin' care of you. Don't you be forgettin' dat. We got rememberin' do. You gonna be rememberin' trust and love for the next little bit. God got da pen now. Trust and love. Dat be da thing now."

"That's all?"

"Dat be plenty, child."

Sarah comes to me from a place of great love. She's a nearly constant loving presence in my life. I've learned to trust her because coming from love, Sarah's advice is worth considering. I don't always follow her guidance, but I've learned to listen, and when I don't follow her suggestions, usually I wish I had.

Music Row

BEFORE I LEFT the farm, I rented a small, furnished house in an old Nashville neighborhood, just a short walk from two universities, kitschy stores, several burger joints, and a bunch of coffee shops.

I arrived in Nashville on April Fool's Day 2012. At the time, I wondered if it was a sign of some sort. I still wonder about it. Actually, I'm pretty sure it was.

I parked in front of my new place, found the key in the lockbox and opened the door. The house was clean and furnished—hardwood floors, plastered white walls and ceilings, mismatched hand-me-down furniture, plastic lamp shades and unadorned windows. It was a place more familiar with day-tripping tourists than come-to-stay seniors.

I dropped my three boxes of stuff in a corner and hauled my suitcase to an upstairs bedroom. I was moved in. I had no plan beyond moving in. *Now what?* I thought.

Maybe I'd do some writing. No one was there to dissuade me, so I opened the cardboard box labeled "office" and stocked the dining table with pens and paper – pens in neat rows, paper stacks aligned with the table edge. Admiring the austerity of my surroundings, I pulled up a chair, sat and picked up a pen.

My mind was blank. I doodled waiting for words to come. Nothing came, so instead of writing a book, I wrote a to-do list: go to grocery store, register car, get new driver's license, get post office box, notify credit card companies and friends of my new address. It was enough to keep me busy for a few days. The list gave me a bit of purpose. I had stuff to do.

Several days later, I was done.

Now what?

I stopped to notice the thought. I had plenty of time for noticing thoughts. *Now what?* was not a thought I'd thought much in my well-organized, list-driven life. There'd always been something more to do. I noticed that I was, for the first time in a very long time, without anything to do and I didn't care for it. The thought made me nervous.

I got up from my chair and stood staring at my three boxes of stuff for a few minutes. I was lost and lonely. I sat down in the middle of the floor, allowed the tears to well up, and sobbed. I even wailed once or twice. I wondered whether I'd ever wailed before. I couldn't remember a time when I'd wailed. I kinda liked it. Wailing made the sobbing feel more sincere.

The sobbing went on for 15 or 20 minutes and stopped as suddenly as it started. I dried my eyes and went to the bathroom. The lost, lonely feeling came back for another visit. I returned to my place on the floor and sobbed some more. The sobbing went on like this, mostly early morning and late at night, for a couple of weeks.

After a few days, I was practiced in the warning signs of weeping. I felt the loneliness rise in me and took my seat on the floor. Waves of sadness rolled through me and I wept. The tears stopped. I blew my nose and enjoyed a few minutes of calm before the sadness crept in again and more tears flowed.

Never in my life had I experienced anything like this. For 60 years, I'd kept my emotions in check. Except for the aftermath of *Harry and Tonto*, I hadn't cried since I was a child.

"Men don't cry," Dad said. I believed him and, being a go-getter, I'd lived by those words...until now.

A part of me knew my weeping was making up for lost time, but because it was so out of character (particularly the wailing), I asked myself over and over if I was nuts.

"You doin' fine, child," Sarah said one day. "Clearin's all. You lettin' go. Makin' room."

"Room? For what?"

There was no answer.

Then one day I woke early, just before dawn. I felt rested and empty. There was no emotion. There were no tears left in me. I lay in bed watching the glow of sunlight creep in around the edges of curtained windows. All was silent except for the hum of cool air blowing through a floor vent beside the bed. Gradually, emptiness gave way to peace.

"Da easy place," Sarah said. "It always here for you, child. You rememberin' how to be in da easy place. Feelin' it."

For the first time in as long as I could remember, I relaxed—no fretting about what I'd left behind, no to-do list, no emotion, no discomfort. My mind was clear. My heart thumped along easily. The knot in my stomach unraveled. The muscles in my arms and legs fell away from my bones.

It was the easy place. Not a thought, but a feeling.

⇥⊨◉ ◉⊨⇤

The phone rang, startling me out of the easy place.

Nobody'd call me so early unless…. Maybe Coco fell. Maybe she had a stroke. Maybe….

My mind conjured a whole list of horribles before I answered, "Hello?"

It was Jenkins, the young woman I'd met in Brazil. We talked about my move, my new digs, and her family for a few minutes before she said,

"Hey, you're right up the street from me. Why don't you hang up and come over for tea?"

Turns out her house was just four blocks away.

A coincidence?

Fifteen minutes later, I walked up the front steps of a cute bungalow painted green with cream-colored trim. It had a big front porch looking out over a tiny front yard and a shady, tree-lined street. It was like the house my grandparents had lived in. It was the kind of house I'd always wanted to live in—small, manageable, and well-kept.

"Come in," Jenkins yelled from somewhere inside. "Door's open."

I stepped inside, looked around and felt a bolt of electricity move through me. Goose bumps erupted all over my body and I knew. I can't explain it, but I knew and I said, "Jenkins, I'm going to live in this house."

She looked at me strangely, then laughed, "Don't think that's going to work. I live here."

"I'm going to buy this house from you."

"I doubt that," she said, smiling. "My husband and I are building a house up the street. You probably walked by it on your way here. I guess it's possible we'd rent the place to you when we move, but we're real estate people. We own several rental houses in the neighborhood. Plenty of college students and faculty want housing around here. We'll *never* sell this place."

"We'll see," I said.

A few months later I rented the house and moved in as Jenkins and her family moved up the street.

A few months after that, I bought it.

Orange Soda

It DIDN'T TAKE long for Coco to adjust to my new life in Nashville. I hear the phone ringing?

"Steve?"

"Yes, Coco. Are you okay? You never call this late."

"Of course, I'm okay. And it's not that late. When are you coming over?"

"I'm not coming over. It's 10 o'clock. I'm getting ready to go to bed. Is your dementia kicking in? I've been wondering when it was going to kick in."

"Don't be starting with the dementia. I'm not having anything to do with the dern dementia. I thought maybe you were coming over."

"And why would you think that? I'm never at your place this late."

"Well, if you're coming over, would you go by the store and get some strawberry ice cream—just a pint. I've been thinking about strawberry ice cream."

"Not tonight, Coco. I'll get your strawberry ice cream tomorrow."

"I like Purity brand. I'd like a little taste before I go to bed."

"I'm beginning to understand that, but I'm not..."

"And I'd like it in a cake cone—one of the little ones. They're in boxes on a shelf at the end of the ice cream aisle. Get a small box of those too."

"Coco, I'm not coming over tonight. I'm standing here next to the bed in my boxer shorts and..."

God's Got The Pen

"You might enjoy a taste too. We could sit at the kitchen table and have some. I can taste it right now."

"Coco, hold that thought and go to bed. I'll get ice cream tomorrow and bring it by."

"Well, if you change your mind, I'll be up for a while. I sure would enjoy..."

And there you have it, my new life with Coco.

For 18 years, I knew her as mom. She did mom things. She was a lot like the other moms in our neighborhood. When we boys were little, she cooked and cleaned and drove carpools and Forsythia-switched us regularly to maintain some semblance of control. During our teen years (when switches lost political favor and their power), she turned to vigilance—hunting tirelessly for evidence of the devil's work. She pulled Playboy magazines from places we knew she'd never look and trashed them with great fanfare. She marked her bourbon bottle to discourage underage drinking. She encouraged my dad to have "talks" with us—lots of them.

She was a mom. I had no idea she was a real person.

Then I was gone for 40 years. I'd visit once or twice a year, but that was about it.

Now I was back, getting to know her in a new way. We had long talks about her growing up as the youngest daughter of an old-time Methodist minister with prohibitions on dancing, playing cards and most anything else a teenage girl could think to do. She waxed eloquent about her college days and raising five boys, the disappearance of one of my brothers and the toll it took on her, a neighbor's suicide, and her endlessly troubled marriage to my dad. She loved to talk about family camping trips we took as kids and the places she still hoped to see someday. Her memory was sharp, way better than mine. She was all about her hair and staying out of the wind. And she had her quirks—like sudden urges for foods she hadn't tasted in a very long time, her penchant for

39

neatness, her closet full of paper towels and feather dusters, her addiction to diet orange soda, and her fear of arriving late to anything.

She regularly talked to God and his helpers.

"Angels," she said. "I'm talking to angels. They're my friends now. Don't you go thinking it's the dementia. It's not the dern dementia."

❧

Wednesday was beauty parlor day. It was a constant in our lives—the weekly event around which everything else orbited. Most weeks, it was the only thing on our calendars. Hear the phone ringing?

"Steve?"

"Good morning, Coco."

"Tomorrow's Wednesday."

"Yes ma'am, I know, and yes, I know it's beauty parlor day, and yes, I'll pick you up early so you won't have to worry about missing your appointment."

"I like to go early," she said, ignoring me.

"I know. We have this conversation every Tuesday. Your appointment is at 2 o'clock tomorrow. I'll pick you up at 1 o'clock and we'll be at the beauty parlor sitting by the receptionist at least a half-hour early. And now is when I say, 'Coco, relax,' knowing full well you won't."

"We could go earlier just to be sure."

"Coco, we'll be there plenty early. I promise. We've never been late for your hair appointment or anything else."

"Well, I'll be ready at noon if you want to go a little earlier."

❧

Coco's health was declining.

"What'd you expect? I'm 89 years old. Things don't work like they used to. Can you do some cooking?"

I started going by to see her most days—taking her the foods she requested. I made potato salad, barbecued chicken, pimento cheese sandwiches on white bread, coleslaw, three-bean salad, macaroni and cheese, roast beef hash, tuna noodle casserole with crumbled potato chips on top, tuna salad, and on and on. She never ate more than a bite of anything but she savored it. Over the next several months, she tasted her way through the equivalent of a 1950's southern cookbook.

She also made a list of things she wanted to remember and added to it regularly. Every visit, she asked me to get her list. We'd talk through it item by item. I'd tell her what I remembered (if I remembered anything at all) and she'd challenge my recollection. Virtually every challenge ended with a dismissal, "That's not right. I'll ask one of your brothers."

And then one day, I found her sitting at the kitchen table looking at old pictures, drinking another diet orange soda. Her skin had turned orange.

"Coco..." I started.

"I know. I know," she said, waving me off. "Too many orange sodas. I keep telling myself to cut back."

"Coco, it's not the orange sodas. It's jaundice. We need to get you to the doctor."

"I feel fine," she said. "It's the orange sodas. I don't need a doctor."

"Well, let's call your doctor and see what he says." I dialed the number for her.

The next morning, we were in his office at 8 o'clock (an hour early). Two days later Coco underwent exploratory surgery and stayed in the hospital overnight while the lab ran tests. I was in her room when the surgeon came to see her with the results. He was young, maybe 40, and had an easy bedside manner. Delivering bad news was part of the job and he did it gracefully.

"Mrs. Johnson, I have the results of the lab tests. You have pancreatic cancer. I'm afraid it's inoperable."

"How long do I have?" Coco brightened.

"A few months, maybe 6 months."

"Oh, thank you!" Coco said, smiling and pushing herself up in her bed. "I'm so glad to know. And I'm ready to go sooner if that's what happens. Thank you, doctor. I'm so grateful."

She held out her arms, inviting him closer. He sat on the edge of her bed and let her give him a hug.

"Now, go on and help your other patients. I know you're busy. I was married to a doctor. I know."

I followed him out the door. In the hallway, he turned to me and said, "Your mom's amazing."

"I know," I said.

⋯⊷⊚ ⊚⊶⋯

Toward the end, Coco lay in a hospice bed. She didn't want visitors other than family and she didn't want much of us. Talk was tiring for her. So I went by in the morning and sat with her for a little while. We watched a pair of cardinals tending their nest in a tree outside her window.

One morning I walked into her darkened room. She lay in bed with her eyes closed—breathing lightly. I sat down. I couldn't tell whether she was awake or not, so I asked, "Coco, are you talking to God?"

"No," she said quietly, "I'm thinking about deviled eggs."

"I can make some if you like."

She opened her eyes.

"Oh, would you? Just a taste's all I want. Will you make *my* deviled eggs?"

"Of course. Yours is the only recipe I know..."

"Drain the pickle relish really good before you put it in. You don't want 'em watery."

"I know, Coco. I know how to make your deviled eggs…"

"And the dry mustard. Colman's. Just a touch. Enough to taste but not too much."

"I know…"

"And don't over boil the eggs. Don't want that sulfur taste."

"Coco, I know how to make deviled eggs."

She closed her eyes and was quiet.

After a few minutes, I said, "Are you talking to God now?"

"No, I'm still thinking about deviled eggs."

"Well, maybe they're the same thing," I said.

She opened her eyes wide and turned a steady gaze on me. Then she sat straight up in her bed. She hadn't done that in weeks.

"I think you might be right," she said.

She smiled brightly, lay back down, closed her eyes, sighed as if she were relaxing into a warm bath and passed away the next morning.

⊷⊷⊷ ⊷⊷⊷

I spent a year with Coco before she died. I knew when I left the farm I was moving to Nashville to be with her. I'm grateful for every minute.

Now what? I thought.

Suddenly my calendar was wide open. What would I do?

A few nights later, I had a dream that's still vivid in my memory.

I was kneeling with several others in an open field of newly mowed grass. (I love the smell of mowed grass.) The sun was bright and the sky was clear. The breeze was pleasantly cool.

Those of us kneeling wore simple white linen robes and waited patiently for an older man to address us. He sat in front of us, reading through some papers. His wing-back chair had seen better days. White stuffing showed itself through the faded flowery fabric on the chair's arms.

The old guy had wispy white hair and a neatly trimmed white beard. His eyes were bright and clear. He wore khaki pants and an old flannel shirt. His reading glasses perched precariously on the tip of his nose.

"Steve," he said, putting his papers down. "Come up here and stand beside me. I'd like to talk to you."

I got up and walked to his chair.

"I have something for you to do," he said, looking at me over his reading glasses.

"Of course," I said. "What is it?"

He smiled.

"The knowledge is within you. Trust your knowing."

"But…"

Before I could ask the next question, I woke up.

That was different, I thought. *Wonder what that was about?*

The Right Way to Live

NEAL AND MY youngest daughter, Anne, put Yoda on a plane to Nashville after I got settled.

My short-legged buddy was back. We walked, sat, ate, and traveled together, but slept in separate bedrooms. (He needed his space.) I loved having him around, but he came with a full coat of hair that seemed to renew itself every few days all over the floor and everywhere else. It gave me purpose. I vacuumed, swept, and dusted up dog hair nearly every day.

For the first time, I washed my own clothes. I learned a lot about bleach, mostly the hard way. I shrunk the unshrinkable. I burned a hole in my portable ironing board—the cover and the board. I slowly gravitated to jeans and t-shirts. I turned my dial to *low maintenance*. The starch literally went out of my life.

I tended a small garden, watched squirrels eat what blossomed, went to the store to buy what the squirrels ate, cooked for myself, and gathered the few daisies the slugs didn't shred to decorate the kitchen counter.

I was tossed into homemaking and gradually acclimated to it. I gained new appreciation for all Neal had done—things I'd taken for granted. I hadn't known how much there was to tending a house and yard. In many ways she'd been my wife, mother, sister and best friend. Now I was becoming my own wife, mother, sister and best friend. I was getting in touch with parts of me I'd not exercised when somebody else was there to play those parts.

"What you rememberin'?" Sarah wanted to know.

"Remembering?"

"Yes, child. What you rememberin'?"

"Don't know," I said.

"Goodness," Sarah said. "You quite da projec', child. You rememberin' how to care fo' yo'self. How to love yo'self."

"I am?"

"Pay attention to what you lovin'. Trust yo'self. Follow yo' heart. You rememberin'."

"Right," I said, without understanding any of it.

Yoda and I fell into an easy routine. I reserved mornings for walks and gardening. Afternoons were for house chores and errands. (It wasn't long before I added a late afternoon nap.) Evenings were for cooking, reading and the occasional dinner out. I discovered I could slow down and love most everything I did, with the possible exception of making up the bed.

I began to *feel* what I loved—what captivated me. Long, easy walks. Trying out new recipes and cooking dinner for friends. Puttering around the garden and arranging flowers in a vase. Admiring newly polished wood floors and the crisp smell of clean sheets. An outdoor shower. Sitting on the front porch in the evening with Yoda, drinking a glass of wine.

I also began to notice what was in the way of what I loved. It took a while, but I finally identified it as *fear.*

"Now we be gettin' somewhere," Sarah said. "We gettin' to da nub o' things. Time fo' rememberin'."

The Meaning of A

LATER THAT EVENING, I sat thinking about *fear*. Was I a fearful person? I'd never thought of myself that way, but if I was, what did I fear? I wasn't coming up with anything until this memory clicked in...

Over 40 years ago, I was a student at The University of Virginia. In my final year as an undergraduate, I took a music seminar taught by the head of the Music Department, Ernest "Boots" Mead.

The seminar met at Mr. Mead's home, in the living room, every Wednesday afternoon. Mr. Mead sat at his grand piano in his tweedy jacket, signature bowtie, and professor spectacles. He played great music and talked about it.

Sounds sort of intellectual and peaceful, doesn't it? Well, it may have been intellectual, but it wasn't peaceful. Mrs. Mead ran the local animal shelter. She was forever bringing injured animals home and nursing them back to health—a big job. She scurried from cage to cage, cleaning, feeding, and doctoring broken appendages, while we listened to great music.

An owl named Harry Bird lived in a gigantic cage in one corner of the dining room. He hooted whenever Mr. Mead played the piano, which meant he hooted his way through our seminar each week.

A hawk recuperated in a cage in another corner of the dining room. He let loose with a high-pitched scream whenever Harry Bird hooted. They were a duet of sorts.

A large rodent lived in a cage on the Meads' dining room table—an unusual centerpiece. He climbed on his exercise wheel and ran for his life whenever the birds of prey hooted and screeched.

Bobbie, a big shaggy dog, and Moses, a short-legged, floppy-eared Bassett Hound, barked and ran circles around the dining room table whenever the rodent exercised.

Occasionally, Clara, a raccoon who lived in the basement, escaped and tore around the house, the dogs on her tail, Mrs. Mead chasing after the dogs.

It was a Dr. Dolittle-kind-of-place. The seminar wasn't peaceful, but it was entertaining.

I had a serious girlfriend at the time and she had a serious mother. After getting to know me over dinner one evening, mother informed daughter that I lacked *prospects*. I was a nice enough young man and adorable bordering on handsome, but I'd never get a decent job. According to her, English majors starved after graduating from college. So did their spouses and children.

This worried mother and began to worry daughter. Some of the worry rubbed off on me. So I went to visit the University's graduate business school. They confirmed what others had told me: if I attended their school and managed to graduate, I'd graduate with prospects. That sounded promising.

There was, however, one small problem, they said. There was no place for me in business school if I didn't spiff up my grades a bit—actually, a lot. I'd have to make an *A* in virtually every class that year, including Mr. Mead's seminar.

Oh, bother, I thought.

So the next week, after our seminar, I told Mr. Mead my sad story. I was a young man without prospects who needed to get some prospects. I had to get a bunch of *A's* before I could get any prospects and therefore needed to get an *A* in his seminar. I asked Mr. Mead how he intended to evaluate us. Would there be papers, quizzes, maybe an exam?

Mr. Mead smiled his wry little smile. "Mr. Johnson," he said. "Yours is indeed a sad story. I haven't thought about seminar grades yet. But I will and I'll get back to you."

Being a normal and right-thinking young man, I assumed he'd address the issue the next week during our seminar, but he didn't. So, after the seminar, I told Mr. Mead my sad story again. I was a young man without prospects, etc., who needed to get an *A* in his class. I asked whether he'd thought about seminar grades yet.

Mr. Mead smiled his wry little smile, again. "Mr. Johnson," he said. "Your story is indeed a sad one. Unfortunately, it does not improve with re-telling. I haven't thought about seminar grades yet. But I will and I'll get back to you."

I'll save us some time now and simply tell you that my conversations with Mr. Mead about getting an *A* in his seminar continued in this unsatisfactory way every week for the next six months. It wasn't until mid-March, perilously close to the end of the school year, that Mr. Mead called me into his office and sat me down.

"Mr. Johnson," he said. "I've decided how I will evaluate your performance in my seminar."

Well, about damn time, I thought.

"I'd like you to write a paper entitled *The Meaning of A.* Write it however long it needs to be and turn it in to me during the first week of May, so I'll have time to read it and get your grade posted."

"But, Mr. Mead," I started, "I don't know what you mean by *the meaning of A.* Exactly what would you like me to write about? How would you like me to…"

Mr. Mead held up his hand and smiled his wry little smile. (His wry little smile was wearing thin.)

"Mr. Johnson, I've said all I have to say on the subject. Go away, employ that fertile mind of yours in serious thought, and write your paper."

"But, Mr. Mead..."

"None of your *buts*, Mr. Johnson. Go on. I've got work to do and so do you."

I left his office shaking my head. I had six weeks to write the paper that would determine whether I'd ever get any prospects and I had no idea what Mr. Mead wanted. He wouldn't tell me what to do. What was this riddle—*the meaning of A?*

The following week, Mr. Mead stopped me as I left our seminar. He asked how my paper was coming.

"It's not," I said. " I've thought about it for an entire week. I have no idea what you want. You need to..."

"Keep thinking," Mr. Mead said, smiling as usual. "I'm sure something will come to you."

The next week, Mr. Mead asked again how the paper was coming.

"Well, it's still not coming," I said. "Mr. Mead, I've thought about *the meaning of A* for two solid weeks. I'm going nowhere. You need to..."

Mr. Mead didn't smile this time. I could tell he was beginning to wonder whether I'd ever get there.

And then, a few days later, in the middle of a sleepless night, a voice came to me—telling some sort of story. At first I didn't know what the voice was talking about, but quickly realized the voice was dictating my seminar paper. It seemed to have some good stuff to say.

Not wanting to disturb the voice, I quietly got out of bed and sat at my desk. For the next few hours I wrote furiously. As the voice faded, I sat back in my chair, exhausted and sleep-deprived, but my paper was written. The heart palpitations subsided for the first time in weeks.

I'd spend a few minutes here telling you about my enlightening paper, but it's not essential to the story. Instead, I'd like to share its last few sentences:

I've been a student for the past 16 years. I've learned a lot.

A few things I've learned too well. I've learned to care a great deal about what others want me to do and what they think of what I do. I wait expectantly for direction and the report cards that tell me how well I've performed. I'm always looking to somebody else for guidance and the next A.

In a few weeks, I'll graduate from this University. Report cards will not come in the mail anymore. I'll have to take responsibility for choosing what I will and won't do, evaluate my own performance, take my own measure of excellence, and determine, for myself, the meaning of A.

I finished my paper. I bought a nice academic-looking folder, put my paper in it, and started for Mr. Mead's office, but I had a nagging feeling there was something more to say.

Along the way it came to me. I stopped, opened the folder, flipped to the last page of my paper, and, below those few sentences you just read, I wrote the following:

Dear Mr. Mead:

Thank you for leading me to this understanding. I will not forget it. Now I go off to learn how to live it. I'll need to make some changes.

And thank you for being my teacher. I'm truly grateful.

And, by the way, I still need an A in your class.

Sincerely,

Steve

"Dat some good rememberin', child. What you feelin'?"

"Surprise and disappointment. Forty years ago I wrote that paper—a paper about my need for approval. As far back as I can remember I cared deeply what others thought of me and I worked hard to do things the right way—to live the right way. Doing what my parents and teachers and other adults told me to do and when I was done, asking for my report card.

"Way back then, I knew I'd need to change the way I saw the world and learn to live in it differently, but I didn't. Rather than do anything differently I went right on trying to live my life the right way and looking to others for approval.

"Why'd I do that? Why has it taken me 60 years to notice? Why do I still have this deep concern about what others think of me? What am I afraid of?"

"I thinkin' you know, child."

Sarah was right. I did.

I wanted to fit in and to fit in I felt I had to do things *their* way. So I did things *their* way even though much of it I found silly, even painful. I'd let go of my dream to be an English professor and a writer and a whole bunch of other things my heart wanted so I could get my American Dream and the approval that came with it. And I got *their* approval and I basked in the glow of it for a day or two before I felt empty.

"Dat good, child," Sarah said. "Yo' body gonna remind you. You'll see."

I began to notice when my heart said go off-grid and go left, but fear said follow the rules and go right. My stomach tightened—really tightened. That was new and I worried about it until I understood it as an alarm begging me to pay attention. When the alarm sounded, I asked myself what I was afraid of. When I looked hard at the fear, I nearly always concluded there was nothing to fear from others or myself. I didn't need to care what others thought and I could easily give myself a pass. I'd do what my heart wanted and quit doing what I felt obliged to do.

That was easier said than done, but slowly I learned to feel the fear of social disapproval as it rose in me, look it in the eye, and walk through it. No fighting it. No running from it. Seeing it and walking through.

I can't remember a time since when I've regretted passing up *the right way to live*. Every time I walked through my fear of what others might think, I found the freedom to be and do what I loved and my stomach relaxed. After a bunch of stomachaches, I came to understand noticing and working with fear as part of my path. I was preparing for something.

"Yes, child," Sarah said. "Time comin' when dis gonna be useful. You gonna face a heap o' skeptics. You gonna raise up fears in folks. Some gonna run from you. Some gonna fight you. Dis only they fear. Let it be. Like you, they rememberin'. They gonna work with fear an' find love in time. Some gonna join up with you and walk with you. You leadin' the way, child. Step forward slow. Bein' aware, not afraid. This be comin'."

"When?" I asked.

"Soon," she said. "When it time. In God time."

And then, a few days later...

"Time to go, child," Sarah said.

"Sorry, but we already went."

"Time for a trip. Got jus' da place. Mo' rememberin'. You fas' trackin' now."

The Woods

I BOOKED A cabin near Sewanee, Tennessee for five days. It was remote—
no phone service, no TV, no internet, in a spot high on a ridge at the
edge of a leafless winter forest. It was eerily quiet. Whatever stillness
I enjoyed in my little Nashville house paled by comparison with the
silence blanketing the woods around me.

"Nice," Sarah said.

The cabin was small. The kitchen, dining area, living room and
bath were tucked into a few square feet on the main floor. The bedroom
was upstairs in the loft. The front porch was furnished with a rickety-
but-serviceable rocking chair and a rustic wooden table. From my seat
on the porch I had an expansive view across the deep valley below the
ridge.

I unpacked and stocked the kitchen, then settled into a threadbare
chair and stared at the electric coil heater standing where the fireplace
had once been. It glowed bright orange. I felt its heat on my knees and
a light, cool breeze on my neck. The cabin's bare-wood walls were not
much of a barrier between nature and me.

"You could have found me a place with insulation," I said aloud.

"You be jus' fine, child."

"And now what do I do?"

"Be quiet, child. Relax. Let dis come to you."

So I sat. I tried to relax, but my mind was racing. What would I
eat for dinner? Did I bring enough food? Was Yoda okay? (I'd left him

with a dog-sitter.) Nobody knew where I was. What if something happened? What if my car broke down out here? Help was a very long way away. Would I be warm enough? The electric fire was the only heat in the place. Maybe I could find some extra blankets somewhere. I'm no pioneer. Maybe Neal was right. Maybe I am prissy. Should I be out here alone? Maybe I better go into town and call somebody to tell him where I am. Who would I call? What difference would it make?...and on and on...

"What dat, child?"

"What?"

"What you thinkin'?"

"Nothing," I said.

"See what you thinkin'."

I sat for a while—thinking about my thoughts.

"Ah," I said, like I'd happened on some major-league discovery. "Fear. It's all fear. Not having enough. Not being safe. Not being comfortable. Not good enough..."

"Now we cookin'," Sarah said.

As I sat in the stillness, memories came. I remembered getting all A's on an 8th grade report card. My dad wanted to know why I hadn't gotten A+'s. I came in second in a high school golf tournament. My dad wanted to know why I hadn't won. I lost a 6th grade girlfriend to another kid in class. I was heartbroken. I couldn't understand why she dumped me, so I asked her. "I like him better," she said.

All afternoon, memories of coming up short flooded my mind. At dusk, my old and now familiar friend, sobbing, overtook me. I sobbed uncontrollably for an hour or so.

I felt unworthy—not good enough.

"This belief holding you back, child. You seein' it and you discoverin' you worthy. You powerful. You rememberin' who you is. You bringin' a gift only you can. You plenty good enough."

After dinner, I went to bed. It was a bitterly cold, foggy night. The loft was so dark I couldn't see my hand in front of my face. The silence was palpable—absolute stillness except for the occasional blood-curdling screech of a screech owl. I lay there in the pitch-black dark for a good while before I fell asleep and dreamed this dream:

I was riding shotgun in a two-seat helicopter. It was my helicopter. I had a pilot. He wore khaki pants and an old flannel shirt. He smiled at me—a kindly older man. He didn't look like much of a pilot and he wasn't. He seemed confused by all the switches on the dashboard and when we finally lifted off, he flew erratically. With every harrowing dip and turn, my heart leapt into my throat.

"What the hell are you doing?" I yelled over the roar of the engine.

"Fun, huh?" he replied.

"Not fun," I screamed to make sure he heard me. "Take me down. Land this thing."

We went straight down and hit the ground hard. I heard a loud *BANG*, but miraculously the helicopter held together and was still running.

"Get out!" I said over the roar of the engine.

"What?" the old man said, smiling. He looked like he might laugh.

"Get out!"

"Oh, okay. As you wish." He smiled at me again, climbed out of the pilot's seat and walked around to take my seat. I scooted over, took the controls and the helicopter lifted off.

"I don't know how to fly this thing either," I said, looking over at the old guy.

"I think you do," he said.

"What? How would you know…"

"Trust yourself. Trust your knowing. You know," he said, smiling.

Suddenly I did know. I realized I'd known all along.

I flew the helicopter easily. It was exhilarating. I didn't know where I was going and I didn't care. I loved flying. I tipped the helicopter this way and that, flying high over snow-capped mountains, then low over treetops following the silver thread of a river...

I woke up.

Damn, I thought. *Just when things were getting interesting.*

"What dat?" Sarah wanted to know.

I didn't hesitate this time.

"I may not know what this adventure is about, but whatever it is, I can handle it. Nothing to fear. I know how to do this."

"You da pilot," Sarah chuckled. "You flyin'."

The next morning, as the sun came up, I happily made myself a cup of coffee and went out on the porch in jeans, heavy wool socks and a sturdy fleece pullover. I felt good. Light fog misted the view. The air was moist and cold. The coffee was hot. A tiny brown bird flew in and perched on the porch railing in front of me. She looked at me, unafraid. Then as quickly as she came, she darted away.

I lapsed into remembering.

Jesus, I thought. *Here we go again.*

My mind clicked through snapshots of my life and the feelings they carried, from my earliest recollections to the present—playing in the creek across the street from my childhood home, the sycamore I climbed in the yard next door, playing kickball on the playground behind the school, fishing with Sarah and my brothers at the farm, a high school trip to Center Hill Lake, college days in Charlottesville, the grind of graduate school, marrying Neal and our early carefree years in Chicago, jogging along the Chicago lakefront, my life as a young lawyer, switching from lawyer to businessman, children, the houses we lived in, the neighborhoods, new friends, family trips, fly-fishing in Montana, cooking with my daughters on rainy Sunday nights in Seattle, moving to the farm, leaving the farm, and picking Yoda up at the airport.

The slide show was long. The remembering went on all day—a life review of sorts. I was surprised when the fog-bound sun disappeared below the ridge in the late afternoon.

Here it came again—the weeping. Another full hour of weeping. I won't bore you with the details. Suffice it to say, I wept for it all—my entire life. The life I'd left behind.

Sarah was back. This time there were no questions.

"Yo' life, child. All you been. All you done. Rememberin' and lettin' go. Clearin' da way for new life. God got da pen now."

I went to bed early again. Remembering and weeping were wearing me out. I fell asleep and dreamed this dream:

I was walking along a dirt road through sagebrush and cactus on a bright sunny day. It was hot and windy. Sand blew around me, smudging my sweat-streaked glasses. I took them off to clean them and instead, dropped them, cracking both lenses and bending the frame. It looked bad.

Oh no, I thought. *My glasses. I've worn these as long as I can remember.*

The dream shifted to a long white counter in an optician's office. The white-haired, old guy behind the counter smiled at me. He looked familiar. He wore a comfortable flannel shirt and khaki pants under his lab coat.

"Time for new glasses," he said, smiling and shaking his head.

He handed me new frames with clear lenses. I put them on. I could see fine—actually, better than I'd seen with the old glasses. I looked in the mirror. The new glasses looked good on me—really good.

"Nice," I said.

I woke up.

Now *I* was asking questions.

"What was that about?"

I heard what sounded like a crowd of people laughing somewhere near the ceiling.

"You seein' better," Sarah said. She was laughing too. "Old way of seein' goin'. New way of seein' comin'. God got da pen. He workin' with you. Follow yo' heart an' trust yo' knowin'."

The third day was about another fear—fear of opening my heart. I remembered the times in my life I'd walked away from love because I was afraid. The memories traced back to the heartbreak of losing my college girlfriend. It was a chest-ripping heartbreak that lasted for months and left a devastating impression on me. I survived it, but I wasn't going to go through that again. So, without knowing it, I'd built an impenetrable wall around my heart and carefully repaired it anytime a stone came loose.

I sobbed so hard that night I had difficulty catching my breath. I sobbed for lost love and all the love I'd avoided so I wouldn't get hurt again.

"I can't do this," I yelled through the weeping. "I want to love, but I can't. I've tried. And every time I try, I end up walking away. Hurting everybody including me. I give up. It's your problem now. If my heart needs opening, you'll have to do it. A crowbar won't be enough. So good damn luck. You're gonna need it."

There was no response.

The fourth day was about fear too—fear of not having enough. I remembered times of worry about money, worry about not getting the stuff I needed to live life the right way and get my American dream, worry about taking care of the stuff once I got it, and realizing late in life I didn't really want any of it. I didn't need it. A simpler life suited me. My fear of not having enough was a waste of time. There was no sobbing about any of this—just disappointment that I'd put so much effort into getting and caring for stuff, I'd missed a lot of living. I shook my head and said, "I get it. Let's move on."

After dinner, I sat to read a book I pulled off the shelf—a book a guest before me had left behind. I opened it but couldn't read. I stared at the electric fire—just stared. Suddenly I saw myself sitting in front of the electric fire. Steve was sitting over there in his chair staring into the orange glow of the electric coils. I was behind him, watching him sit. That was odd. I could see thoughts passing into and out of his head—so many thoughts, so much noise. And I felt something—the same feeling I'd experienced in my vision of all the broken people surrounding me in Brazil. It was compassion and this time it was for Steve.

He's doing the best he can. I thought. *Trying so hard. Like everybody else. He's a good guy,* I thought, and felt a tear roll down my cheek.

"Good," Sarah said. "Love yo'self, child. Won't be no lovin' anybody else till you love yo'self."

⋆►█◉ ◉█◄⋆

I woke the next morning to sunshine. I felt calm and rested. My mind was strangely quiet. I took my coffee out to the porch, sat for a minute, and walked in my socks to the edge of the ridge. The view was spectacular. I sat down on a big rock and let the warm sun shine on me. No remembering. Just sitting. Making a new slide in a new slideshow. A trickle of what felt like electricity moved through me, from the top of my head to the tips of my toes. It felt good. I had goose bumps all over.

What's that? I wondered.

"Time to go," Sarah said. "Welcome to yo' new life."

I walked back to the cabin and packed my things. I picked up the pen and notepad I'd left on the dining table.

Better make a list before I go, I thought. *Things I love. Things I want to do when I get home. If I'm gonna love myself, I better get on it.*

I felt like a go-getter again.

"Whoa, child," Sarah said. "You does love a list. No harm in lookin' ahead, but don't get yo'self all caught up in it. You got big fish to fry. Things you ain't seen yet. Let 'em come to you. No chasin'. Let 'em come."

I had the car packed—ready to go home—before Sarah spoke up again, "I always here, child. Watchin' over you. I be steppin' back now. Others comin' to hep you. You in good hands. You in da best hands they is. God got da pen, child. Trust and love. Dat be da thing."

That was the last conversation I'd have with Sarah for a while. I didn't know what she meant about stepping back, but it was what it was. I'd know when I needed to know and not before.

All About Me

BACK HOME IN Nashville, I sat at my kitchen counter, drinking a cup of coffee, listening to public radio. The Sunday paper lay in a rumpled pile next to my legal pad. I write my list on a legal pad and every Sunday I make a new list. It's an old habit. I enjoy making my list.

"Ah," a new voice said. "Making your list. Steve loves his list, doesn't he?"

I wasn't born yesterday. I know when I'm being baited. Instead of answering, I wrote on my legal pad: Tuesday 3:00 Plumber.

"Got any messages for me?" I asked.

"We'll come up with something," she said. "What would you like to hear?"

"I don't know," I said.

This time I didn't see the bait dangling in front of my nose.

"Something special," I said.

"Good. Could we tell you you're special and skip the specifics?" she asked.

"Sarah told me long ago we're all special."

"You are. We all are."

"Then being told you're special doesn't really have much punch, does it? It's not special."

"What if we told you you're a divine being?"

"But we're all divine beings."

"Yes, we are."

"Well that's great but I'm talking about a message just for me."

"Okay," she said. "You're a one-of-a-kind divine being."

"We're all unique," I said.

"How true," she said. "That's pretty special, isn't it?"
She laughed.

"How about telling you you're on your spiritual path?" she said.

"We're all on our spiritual paths."

"Also true," she said. "Are you starting to notice a pattern?"

Jeepers, I thought. *Another fucking lesson.*

"Never mind," I said. "Let me finish my list. We're not getting anywhere."

"Oh, but we are," she said. "Who's asking for messages?"

"I am," I said.

"And what does Steve want to hear? That he's more special than anybody else? Or the most special one? The most divine one? The chosen one? The second coming? That Steve's opening to his great purpose? That what's coming will surpass his wildest expectations? What exactly does Steve want to hear?"

"That's a start," I said. "Is this a trick question?"
She laughed again.

"Yes, it is," she said. "But who's playing the trick on whom?"
I thought for a minute.

"Good lord," I said.

"Exactly," she said.

"You said *we* a while ago. Who's *we*?" I asked.

"We'll get to that soon enough."

"Okay. Thanks for the lesson, but I need to finish my list now."
I wrote: Wednesday 8:30 Dentist.

→══◎ ◎══←

The new voice was feminine. It was soft and loving, but direct. It was familiar. The banter was also familiar. I'd soon learn why.

The Road

My DREAMLIFE CAME to life. My dreams were growing clearer, seemingly longer, and more easily remembered. I began to remember many of them in detail.

In one of the early ones, I stood on the side of a dirt road on a bright sunny day in a meadow dotted with wildflowers. I felt the sun on my arms and the warm breeze on my face. The road went up a softly rounded hill past a tall shade tree. I couldn't see over the hill, but the tree's shade was inviting.

I had a brown-paper lunch sack in my left hand. I looked in it. A turkey sandwich—plain turkey between two slices of brown bread, wrapped in wax paper. I was hungry and the tree's shade was calling. I wished there was something more on the sandwich but it'd have to do. It was all I had.

Oh well, I thought. *I'll eat when I get to the tree.*

As I walked, an elderly woman in a long blue dress appeared at my side. She looked familiar but I couldn't recall her name. Before I could ask, she handed me a small white-paper bag. "For your sandwich," she said smiling, and disappeared. I looked in the bag—lettuce, tomato slices, and pickles.

I walked on up the hill. A young man in jeans and a white t-shirt appeared in front of me. He was barefoot. He too looked familiar and had a small white-paper sack for me. "For your sandwich," he said, and disappeared. The sack contained packets of brown mustard, salt and pepper.

I walked on, nearing the top of the hill where a beautiful young woman met me. She wore a flowing white gown. I was drawn to her. I was sure I knew her but I couldn't place her. She handed me a cup of water.

"A little early for wine," she said, smiling.

She disappeared.

At the top of the hill, a colorful quilt lay on the grass in the shade of the tree. No one was there. Just me. I sat down on the quilt and saw the road ahead winding downhill through another long meadow and up another hill. I couldn't see beyond the next hill.

I drank a sip of water, opened the sacks I'd been given and dressed my sandwich. It looked good and I was hungry.

Before I could take a bite...I woke up.

I lay in bed remembering the dream. I heard cheering and laughing. My dark bedroom was full of unseen folks cheering and laughing.

"Where's your sandwich?" the new voice asked.

"I wish I'd gotten to eat it."

"You will. In time."

There was a pause.

"You're on your path. You have most of what you need. It resides within you. What you don't have will be provided along the way. We are here. Always here."

"Thank you," I said. "Where am I going?"

"You see as far ahead as you need to see. Allow the adventure to unfold for you. Let it come to you. I'm here beside you. Always beside you."

"Who are you?" I asked.

The room was suddenly quiet—no more cheering or laughing. I was alone with the mysterious, but familiar, voice.

"You know me well," she said softly. "We go back a long way. Trust your knowing and sleep well."

That dream introduced a theme I'd see represented in other dreams, paintings and journaling—walking a road alone, day or night, up a hill or around a bend where a lone tree stands by the road beckoning me forward, wondering what's over the hill or around the bend but seeing only the road right in front of me.

Coming to Jesus

I'M SITTING AT a small table in Bongo Java, a funky coffee shop near my house. I've been putting this off—wondering whether I'd write this chapter and if so, how far I'd go with it.

I'm looking out the window, sipping my coffee. A man is crossing the street. He's wearing a green t-shirt with the word FEAR on the front. (Stuff like this happens all the time.)

Yep. Fear's what I'm working with right now.

I've recently discovered my fear of what others think of me is overshadowed by my fear of missing what I've come to do in this life. One fear trumps another.

Part of living this life fully is living it openly, honestly and lovingly and that includes telling my story—all of it. So, here's part of my story.

I'm a human incarnation of my soul (just as you're an incarnation of yours). My soul has incarnated on the Earth as other personalities, including Jesus, the Buddha, St. Patrick, a young Mayan princess I call Maya, a Hopi shaman who remains a mystery to me, Hildegard of Bingen, St. Francis, and Leonardo da Vinci. They are part of my soul family.

I mention these eight personalities now because they're important to what I've come to do in this life as Steve.

The rest of this book is about remembering who I am and why I'm here—again.

Mary Magdalene

"YOU KNOW ME," she said.

It was the new voice.

"You've said that before. You seem familiar, like the young woman in my dream."

"Nice," she said.

"So how do I know you?"

"We're coming to that, over the next hill. Maybe wine instead of water this time," she laughed. "And just so you know, you're opening to your great purpose. I believe you wanted to hear that."

"Good to know," I said.

Shortly after my dream about the road and the tree and lunch, I came to understand the new voice was Mary Magdalene. I call her M.

I'd hear her name somewhere—church for example—and my body would light up like a Christmas tree with pleasant electricity. I'd see her name in a book and my body would twitch involuntarily. Lying on a treatment table receiving the healing touch of one of my healers (more on this later), my healer would say something like *Mary Magdalene is here with you*. My body would tingle all over.

At some point, her presence was undeniable.

She became my easy, familiar companion.

"Welcome back," she said.

"What?"

There was no response.

Jeans and a T-Shirt

I SAT WITH my cup of coffee, staring at a painting on the wall above the sofa in my tiny sunroom. I love the painting. A woman in a large golden sunhat is picking red tulips in a field full of them. It reminds me of life in the Pacific Northwest.

Suddenly a young guy wearing jeans and a white t-shirt appeared, lounging on the sofa, bare feet resting on the coffee table between us. He had a nice tan. His hair was short and dark. He looked at me smiling. His eyes were a piercing light blue.

"Jesus," I said.

"Good," he said.

"The jeans and t-shirt threw me for a second."

He laughed easily.

"I'm wearing what you're wearing."

He was right.

"Low maintenance," he said, smiling.

"So, why are you here?"

"I'm you," he said. "Where else would I be?"

He smiled again and faded away.

I sat and sipped my coffee for a minute while my brain strained to comprehend what'd happened.

Okay, I thought. *I'm delusional. Time to check myself into the psychiatric ward.*

"Maybe not," M said.

"What was that about?" I asked.

"What do you think it was about?"

"I knew him right away. There was no question…"

"He likes brown mustard on his turkey sandwiches," she chuckled.

"Ah, the dream."

"Nice," she said. "What did he say to you?"

"He prefers jeans and…"

"After that," she pushed.

"He said he was me."

There was a long pause while M let that sink in.

"That can't be true. Can it?"

"Welcome back," she said brightly.

I heard a crowd laughing uproariously somewhere in the distance.

Over the next several days, the thought *I was Jesus* came and went as quickly as I could push it away. The harder I pushed, the clearer the thought came. One morning, I walked to Fido, another nearby coffee shop. I sat on a stool looking out the window to the street.

Could this be true? Jesus? Really?

Right in front of me a car pulled out of the alley beside the coffee shop to merge into traffic. The front license plate read JESUS. My body jerked like I'd stuck my finger into a light socket. The electricity was quick and powerful.

Okay I thought. *Maybe. I guess it's possible.*

My body jerked again. Electricity pulsed through me—goose bumps everywhere.

"Good lord," I said aloud.

"Exactly," M laughed. "You're remembering."

"I am?"

"Trust your knowing and notice your recent experiences with what you call electricity. You're opening to your purpose. A new energy moves through you. We'll talk about it when it's time."

I walked all day, trying to calm my mind. I was stewing. The Jesus mystery was screwing with my brain and what was this stuff about a new energy?

That night, somewhere in the middle of the night, I lapsed into a dream and found myself walking through a large open stone gate in a thick stone wall. I turned left onto a cobblestone street, high stone walls on both sides. It led to a huge stone building with magnificent wooden doors. They were closed. There was nobody around—just me. I walked toward the doors wondering what was inside.

The doors towered above me and were very heavy. I managed to open one door enough to slip inside and found myself in a cavernous domed room lit from above by a bright circular skylight hundreds of feet above my head. It seemed to open to the sky.

Massive stone walls and marble columns supported the magnificent dome. I stepped to the center of the rotunda and stood in a circle of inlaid marble. I heard a choir singing. Their voices were ethereal. Their music surrounded me. Electricity—what M called a new energy—flowed through me from the top of my head to my toes—exquisite, gentle, and loving. Every cell in my body vibrated. I had goose bumps again.

"Look up," M said.

The dome extended into the heavens. Through the grand skylight, I noticed brilliant white clouds moving across the pale blue sky. The choir, robed in white gowns and light-blue stoles, stood singing in rows, one above the other, in ever smaller circles all the way up the inside of the dome.

The scene was breathtaking.

I woke up.

I lay in bed replaying the dream. It was vivid in my memory and like so many things, familiar. I'd been to this place and I'd go to this place again. I knew it.

"Remembering," M said, cryptically. "Your dreams provide direction. Trust your knowing and follow your heart. You'll find your way."

"What is this? Some kind of cosmic scavenger hunt? A little hint here, another one there? Wouldn't it be a lot easier to tell me what I need to do and help me get on with it?"

M laughed. "Enjoy the adventure. It's all an adventure. Not knowing is what keeps you going. It's part of who you are. Always trying to see over the hill. I've both loved this about you and wished it away."

"So the Jesus thing is real?"

"It is."

"And that means...you and I...we..."

M laughed again. There was more cheering from somewhere near the ceiling of my bedroom.

"Yes, it does," she said.

⋯⊨◉ ◉⊨⋯

A few days later on a hot summer morning, I walked down Nashville's Music Row to another of my favorite coffee shops. I ate an omelet and drank a cup of coffee while I watched the music crowd mingle at tables around me. I felt lonely.

Here came a sprinkling of energy. It tingled through my body.

"What do you need?" Jesus asked.

"A girlfriend," I said.

"At your age?"

"I'm not dead yet. Looking at all the beautiful people. Sitting here by myself. I'm one of the lonely people—Eleanor Rigby."

"I remember. Walking alone can be challenging. You won't walk alone much longer. Must be nice to have a libido at your age."

"I'm sure you had one too."

"Not at your age," he laughed.

"Why...."

I caught myself.

"Oh, right. Sorry. I forgot that part."

"No problem."

"So, if I'm here now and I was you then, am I going to..."

"No," he chuckled. "I did that for all of us, remember? One crucifixion was enough."

"Good to know," I said. "Thanks."

"Want to talk about a girlfriend now?" he asked.

"Maybe not," I said. "Being lonely doesn't seem like such a big deal anymore."

⟶▭◉ ◉▭◀⟵

And that's the way it went. That's the way it still goes. Fleeting encounters with that other life—conversations, seemingly serendipitous events, sprinklings of energy (some stronger than others), dreams, visions, my paintings, my journaling. It has taken time and a lot of these experiences to build trust in me—particularly when it comes to *the Jesus thing*.

I was born a skeptic. Skepticism has served me well. It still serves me. But at some point, the point's been made so many times the skepticism loses its battle with trust. The dream of standing in the center of a light-filled rotunda looking skyward would lead me to the last bit of affirmation I'd need to trust *the Jesus thing*. More on that later.

It's over the next hill, or maybe the one after that.

Touch Me, Heal Me

"IT'S TIME," M said. "You have a gift to deliver. Time to prepare."

"What gift? And what preparation?" I asked. "I keep hearing about a gift but I have no idea…"

"You're the healer," M said.

"What? The healer? You can't be serious. I don't think…"

I suddenly remembered my trip to Brazil where I had a vision of standing in the midst of a huge assemblage of damaged people moving toward something unseen. I had a fleeting thought then I'd be doing healing work.

"Yes," M said. "Your vision. Let this come to you. It's time."

For the next few weeks I heard off and on from M about healing. She explained my healing work would facilitate something called *apotheosis*. I, of course, had no idea what the word meant so I looked it up. It means *elevation to divine status*. My healing work—allowing a new energy to move through me—would open those touched by it to their divinity. At the time, I wasn't sure what that meant either but it sounded like a good thing.

To prepare for this work, I'd need to see several different healers myself. M led to me Bonnie, a long-time Healing Touch practitioner. Then I was asked to see Sandy, a Craniosacral therapist—the best in town many people told me. And then to Ramona, a massage therapist who incorporates energy work into her practice. And then to Jule, a dreamwork coach and Healing Touch practitioner.

By mid-2013, I was seeing at least one of these healers every week. In each session, I learned a bit more. I was being prepared to receive a new energy, store it, and release it to facilitate apotheosis in those open to receiving it.

"Like a battery?" I asked, expecting M to answer.

"Somethin' like dat," Sarah said. "You gettin' ready."

"You're back," I said.

"Yes, child. Wasn't never gone. Jus' stepped back fo' a while's all."

Sarah told me other lives in my soul family would come forward as Jesus had. They'd assist me in the work—bringing their wisdom and their capacity for carrying the energy.

"Yo' hep," Sarah said. "You gonna need hep."

With growing understanding of my healing work, people would try to convince me to join their cause—use the energy to support their group.

"You's no groupie," Sarah said. "All dem boxes too small. You's non-denominal. You bringin' change to everbody."

"Non-denominational," I said. "Are you sure you're a muse?"

"You forgettin', child. Beggars don't get no choosin'."

After a few months of acclimating to my own healing, I was asked to sign up for Bonnie's Healing Touch class.

"Really?"

"Really," M said.

"Okay. I see her next week. I'll ask. But I have to say, I think you've got the wrong guy."

"We don't and you won't have to ask," M laughed. "Let this come to you."

The next week, I walked into Bonnie's treatment room and before I could say anything, she said, "I've been asked to offer you my Healing Touch classes. My next beginner class is in a couple of weeks."

This time I laughed. I told her about my conversation with M.

"Yes," she nodded, smiling. "I know."

"What's this about?" I asked.

"Don't know," she said.

"There's a lot of *not knowing* going around."

She smiled, "Yes, there is."

Back to School

WE MET AT Bonnie's house on a weekend in late October 2013. There were three students in the class, plus Bonnie and three other Healing Touch practitioners who were there to assist.

After a brief introduction, we were doing healing work—no messing around. Bonnie's a certified nurse. She's been a Healing Touch practitioner and teacher for nearly 30 years. She jumps right in.

My first practice partner was Anne. Like Bonnie, she's been a healer for many years.

"You're a brave soul," I said.

In my first experience playing healer, Anne sat in a straight-back chair and I stood behind her. Bonnie asked me to put my hands on Anne's shoulders. As I did, an overpowering flow of energy entered the top of my head, moved through my upper body, down my arms, and through the palms of my hands. I'd felt energy before but this time it was far stronger. I was about to fall down, so I sat down. The energy flow subsided. Bonnie asked if I was okay. I was, as long as the flow of energy wasn't knocking me off my feet. When I could stand again, I put my hands back on Anne's shoulders. The energy flow resumed—strong but manageable this time. A few minutes later, Bonnie asked me to step back and sit down to rest, but Jesus intervened and encouraged me to keep my hands on Anne's shoulders.

I shrugged and nodded at Bonnie, who didn't need an explanation. I stood behind Anne with my hands on her shoulders as the energy ran until it slowed and Jesus suggested I lift my hands. I sat down and relaxed as the energy dissipated.

Bonnie smiled and nodded. It was obviously a powerful experience. Nobody said a word till Anne turned in her chair and looked at me. "You have a gift," she said.

The next day, we were back at Bonnie's. Late in the afternoon toward the end of class, Bonnie asked me to demonstrate a healing procedure on one of the other students. There were lots of pieces to it and I'd only seen it performed once by Bonnie before I stepped up to do it myself.

This'll be interesting, I thought.

My practice partner lay face up on the treatment table and closed her eyes. Bonnie put on some soothing music. The room was quiet.

Jesus asked me to place my hands on my partner's feet. I was suddenly focused intently on her—barely conscious of other people and the room around us. My mind was surprisingly still.

Then came the energy—nearly overpowering. I stepped back from the table and took several deep breaths before putting my hands back on her feet. The energy flowed through me in great pulses.

"Hold lightly," I heard Jesus say. "Easy. Relax. Breathe."

As I followed instructions, my partner shook violently and nearly lifted off the table several times. For whatever reason, her shaking didn't surprise me.

"Don't worry. She's fine," Jesus said. "This is part of her healing. Just what's needed. No more, no less."

As I grew more comfortable, the healing became a dance. I listened to Jesus' direction but found I could play—feeling and moving with the flow of energy. The more I allowed the dance to carry us, the more beautiful and effortless the healing was—blissful and deeply satisfying.

"Nice" Jesus said. "Beautiful. Graceful. Didn't know you could do this, did you? You can. You're remembering who you are. With this, you can do anything. I'm here to help. I'm always here. Trust your knowing.

That's good. Beautiful. Now move to her head and place your hands on her temples. That's it. Hold there. Okay, move on slowly now. Gracefully. Feel the energy moving through you. Go with the flow of it..."

Suggestions came in this way throughout the healing.

Occasionally I felt tired and heard again, "Step back. Feel the earth under you. Breathe. That's good. Take care of yourself. Okay now, let's move forward"....and I was dancing with my partner again—Jesus calling the tune.

When the session ended, my partner lay quietly on the table. I felt the energy subside. The music stopped. All was profoundly silent and I was spent. Unsteady on my feet, I sat down.

Bonnie walked across the room, looked at me, smiled and said, "Wow."

There was nothing more to say. We all had tears in our eyes. *Sacred* is not a word I use often, but the moment felt sacred.

Afterward, Anne said she saw light-filled beings surrounding my partner and me and white light pulsing from the palms of my hands. Others nodded. They'd seen what Anne saw. Bonnie said the light beings called themselves a *host of holies*. She described hundreds of translucent, robed beings surrounding my partner and me—golden light glowing around their heads. The experience was, for all of us, otherworldly.

That class changed the course of my life. It was the first time I understood I was a healer. I didn't see the white light or the robed beings, but I felt the energy and got a lot of help. That was plenty.

As I drove home, Sarah showed up.

"You dancin' with the A-team now, child. Don 't you be forgettin' who you is."

Getting Fixed

It was a beautiful day—sunny and cool. I was comfortably back in my winter garb—jeans, t-shirt and fleece pullover (the one Neal wanted to throw away). I made coffee and sat on the porch.

Sitting on a porch is one of the few things I do well.

Yoda lay sleeping at my feet.

It doesn't get better than this, I thought.

With Halloween just around the corner, carved pumpkins decorated houses up and down the street. Fake spider webs hung from bushes and plastic skeletons pushed up among leaves littering the ground. Bedsheets dangled from the ceiling fan on the porch across the way. A gathering of crows cackled in the trees next door, adding a nice touch. I surveyed my little corner of the world and pronounced it good. I took great comfort in Halloween. It came every year on the same day. It was reliable.

Except for Halloween, I'd arrived at a place of near-perfect uncertainty. I'd left much of the past behind. My overweening desire to manage the future wasn't working. I was stuck in *what was,* and suddenly *what was* was all there was.

"A feather on the breath of God," M said.

"Delighted you reminded me."

M laughed easily. "Hang onto your sense of humor. It'll be useful."

"How so?"

"There's humility in humor. Yours is disarming. Let it work for you."

"Can we talk about yesterday?"

"Sure," M said.

"Where are we going with this? The healing I mean?"

"Trying to see over the hill?"

"I guess."

"Where would you rather be than where you are? Here on your porch. Right now?"

"Jesus," I said. "It's hard to get a straight answer."

"Exactly," she said.

As if on cue, Yoda got up and looked at me.

"Aroooooooo," he said.

"Okay, okay. Back to real life."

Yoda waddled to the porch steps and stood by his leash where I'd left it hanging on the rail.

⊷═◐ ◑═⊷

It was a new beginning of sorts. Over the next year I saw my healers and took more of Bonnie's classes. I was being prepared—in manageable bites—to carry more and more energy. My body adjusted to new energy levels as we went, but it wasn't always happy. After each shift, it complained. Sometimes I felt like I had the flu. Sometimes I was light-headed and off-balance. Sometimes fatigue knocked me down and I took to my bed. Sometimes I ate voraciously for a couple of days and padded barefoot around the house. Sometimes I just felt *off*.

"Let it be," M said, reassuringly. "Your body knows what to do."

After months of energy shifts, I relaxed. Whatever the symptoms, they passed within a few days. These shifts became part of my new normal.

While this was happening, I spent more time practicing healing on friends—some more willing than others. Most were skeptical—some so skeptical they didn't want anything more to do with me and drifted away. Their skepticism became another part of my new normal.

"Their fear," M said. "You're a disruptive force. It's part of who you are. You shake the lives of others—particularly those closest to you. This is just the beginning. There'll be skepticism and jealousy. Many will leave you. It's their opportunity to work with fear and discover there's nothing to fear. Let it be."

Even so, in crept my worry about what others thought of me. I saw it because it was impossible to miss. The skepticism and jealousy of friends were challenging, but I kept going.

"You've faced this many times," M said. "Let it be."

⊷⊷◉ ◉⊷⊷

One day, M asked if I was ready to build my cottage.

"Cottage?"

"The cottage you've been planning."

"Really?"

"Yes," M said. "It's time."

"Why now?"

"You have things to do in your cottage."

That struck a sympathetic chord. All my life I've longed for a small, rustic cottage on a deserted beach. As a kid, I drew pictures of it. During my business career, I flew a lot. On long plane rides, I sketched my cottage many times, floor plans and all. Sketching it felt like an escape.

"Your cottage will be your retreat for a while—a place to recharge—and a place of healing. You'll see. Time to build."

"Where?"

"How about your backyard? You'll want a nice garden too."

"Who's paying for this?" I asked.

"Trust your knowing," M said.

Today the cottage sits quietly in the backyard in a garden full of colorful flowers. It's a peaceful place—exactly what I'd imagined, minus the beach.

One day, in the midst of cottage construction mayhem, I got a call from Caroline. Like me, she was a student in Bonnie's classes. She asked if she could come over.

"Of course," I said. "I'll put on a pot of water."

We sat on the porch and talked, drinking ginger tea. She told me her story. I told her mine. She said she felt *led* to ask whether I'd like to do healing work with her, as her partner. She was familiar and easy to be around. I was remembering how to trust *familiar*.

"Sure," I said. "Let's give it a try."

At first, we practiced on each other. She had a treatment table in a sun-filled, spare bedroom in her house. We traded places on the table and the energies flowed naturally between us. Sometimes mysterious things happened...

"Whoa," Caroline said, stepping away from the table where I lay shuddering. "What was that?"

I don't know," I said. "But it was powerful. My body's vibrating like a tuning fork."

I'd just felt a blast of air blow through me from right to left.

"It felt like wind," I said.

"It blew my hair..."

Caroline paused.

"The breath of God," she said. "I'm hearing it was the breath of God."

"Really?" I said.

Sarah stepped forward, laughing. "You one heavy feather, child."

We learned from this and other *experiences* that we were sometimes feeling the same energies and hearing the same things. Soon others came to lie on Caroline's table or the one we set up in the cottage when it was ready. As promised, the cottage became a place of healing.

In each healing session, Caroline and I worked together. As we stepped up to the table, we heard *let's dance* and we did. I knew where she was and where she'd move next. She knew the same about me. The dance of healing was effortless, like we'd done this before and been partners all along.

"Trust your knowing," M said.

That's the way it was for a couple of years—classes, practice healing sessions, and almost-weekly energy adjustments.

"Gettin' ready," Sarah said.

And then, one day, in the middle of a healing session in the cottage, I was asked to step back.

"Leave this to Caroline. Time to go," M said.

"Go?"

"Watch her work. She has a beautiful gift. Enjoy this moment—an ending and a beginning."

I sat down and watched Caroline move gracefully—still dancing—around the table.

"The laying on of hands," M said.

And that was it. My table work ended, but Caroline and I would dance on—sometimes together, sometimes apart. She was becoming an amazing spiritual healer and one of my dearest friends.

"Time to walk," M said.

"Where?"

"Wherever your heart leads you. Your presence is all that's needed. Trust your heart. It knows the way."

Reading Tea Leaves

OVER THE LAST 7 years, I've experienced differing energy flows enough times to develop a sense of their meaning. As I understand it, the energy is love—the life force—expressed in various ways.

Affirmation—Energy flows through the top of my head into my upper body. It's a *yes*. It can be a light *yes* or a strong *yes*. Sometimes it's so strong I jerk involuntarily in response.

Noticing—Light energy tingling at the top of my head says *pay attention*. Notice something.

Protection—Rarely, I feel powerful energy filling the air around me. It says *be aware*. (It does not say be afraid. I'm never encouraged to be afraid.) It seems to turn threats away or lessen their impact. Thankfully, I haven't had enough experience with this to say much more.

Embrace—I am loved. Sometimes I am simply embraced. Warming energy flows around my body.

Rejuvenation—Energy flows steadily from the Earth up through the bottoms of my feet to the top of my head. It steadies and invigorates.

Adjustment—As my preparation to carry the transforming energy has progressed, I've experienced intense, sometimes debilitating flows of energy. I sit or lie down so I don't fall down.

Transformation—This is the energy of apotheosis. I'm told it's high frequency and quite powerful. I feel its power but the energy feels smooth to me—soft and smooth. It flows from my heart all over my body and beyond, but most intensely through the palms of my hands.

I'm told it goes where it's needed. I'm also told it flows best when I'm quiet and relaxed. "You do your best work when you're asleep," M sometimes says.

⋆⊷⊚ ⊚⊶⋆

I love gardening. I have a number of house plants, including several orchids. They seem to like the light in the cottage. Several months ago, one of the orchids started dropping its flowers—perfectly normal. It dropped all but one of them. It held tightly to a bloom that had withered a week or more before—not normal.

"See how the orchid holds tenaciously to the withered flower?" M asked.

I'd watched the bloom hang by a single thread of desiccated stem for several days.

"The orchid only lets go when there's no energy or life force left to hold the bloom. The human ego is like that, holding onto old habits and ways of seeing the world until there is no life force to support them. As the divine self emerges, the life force lends its support. The ego loses support. There's no energy for holding onto old ways of seeing. Old patterns fall away. This is the change you undergo now. The energy coalesces around your divinity and brings it to bloom. This is apotheosis. This is the healing you bring yourself, others and the All."

Moving Right Along

I HEARD A noise in the kitchen.

Yoda, I thought.

It was 3 o'clock in the morning. I got out of bed to check on things. Yoda was getting on in years and sometimes wandered in the night.

I walked into the kitchen. A woman stood by the refrigerator holding two brown suitcases, one in each hand. Tall and slim with dark hair and brown eyes, she wore a plaid pleated skirt and a yellow sweater. Soft white light illuminated the air around her. She looked as surprised to see me as I was to see her.

"Allow her to come to you," M said.

I didn't approach her, but said, "Is there something I can help you with?"

No answer. She looked around and found Yoda sleeping on the rug just beyond the kitchen.

"Your companion," she said. "Yoda?"

Her voice was soft and gentle.

"Yes. Do I know you? What's your name?" I asked.

"You know me," she said. "What would you call me?"

Without thinking, I said, "Grace."

"I like that," she said.

"Can I help you with your bags?" I asked, stepping forward.

She startled and disappeared.

As my preparation progressed, I experienced more and more of these vivid visions—so vivid I was often confused when I woke up, wondering what was *real*. Occasionally, my day was interrupted by what I called waking dreams and the same question popped up. What was *real*?

"Both and all," M said. "All is your experience. Part of your remembering. No moment more or less real than another. Every moment is awakening."

"Okay," I said, letting the words sink in.

"We are on the same journey," she went on. "All are on the same journey. Our paths are different—each path unique. But the journey is the same. Honor all of it."

As the number of brightly vivid dreams increased, waking and sleeping lost meaning.

"Okay then, who was the young woman with the suitcases?" I asked, expecting M to answer.

"You call me Grace."

By now, new voices weren't a surprise to me. Like the dreams, I took them in stride—yet another part of the new normal.

"So, if you don't mind my asking, what's your real name?"

"Part of your remembering," she said.

"Not you too…"

"Yes. Me too," she said, laughing softly.

Over the next few months, Grace came and went, an easy new presence in my life. She was particularly interested in healing and liked to talk about it.

One day, out of the blue, she said, "Time for a trip."

"What trip?"

"We're going home together."

"What?"

Over the next few weeks, St. Francis and Italy popped up in conversations, ads on my computer, travel shows on TV, and the Sunday newspaper. The signs were everywhere and every time one appeared I felt an energetic nudge—palpable and sweet, but somewhat insistent. Both Grace and M encouraged me. "Your heart knows the way," they said.

Assisi

A COUPLE OF months later, I lay on Sandy's table while she prodded spots on my thick skull. We talked about my upcoming trip to Italy—just days away.

My oldest daughter, Austen, planned the trip. She loves to travel and plan vacations and she's good at it. I'd fly to Rome, drive to Orvieto for a two-night stay, then to Volpaia for a week's walking in the Tuscan hills, and back to Rome for a couple of days before flying home.

"Oh," Sandy said, mildly surprised. She stopped working on my head.

I stopped talking.

"There's someone here for you."

"Who?"

"I'm told you know," Sandy said.

"St. Francis? His name's been popping up everywhere the last few days. Lots of coincidences."

"They're not coincidences," Sandy said. "He's nodding his head. Yes, it's Francis."

"Goodness," I said. "I'm delighted but why is he here?"

(Things like this happen all the time on Sandy's table—part of the new normal.)

"He's waiting."

"For what?"

"An invitation."

"He's welcome anytime," I said.

Suddenly, a tremendous rush of energy flooded my body. I shivered like I'd just emerged from a dip in the Baltic Sea.

"Beautiful," Sandy said. "He's moved into your heart. So beautiful, Steve. I'm so grateful. So grateful to be here for this."

She had tears in her eyes.

The next day, a friend recommended a book, *Eager to Love: The Alternative Way of Francis of Assisi* by Richard Rohr.

More Francis. He's everywhere, I thought.

I bought the book and didn't put it down till I'd read it through. I was taken with it.

While I read, Jesus spoke up. I hadn't heard from him in a while. "Francis is part of who you are now," he said. "I came to teach. Francis came to live the teaching. Now you come in your way."

And then just a day or two before my trip...

"Sorry for the last minute change, Dad. Your flight to Rome canceled," Austen sighed. "You've been rerouted. It's going to work out, but I'll need to rearrange your itinerary so you can get to Volpaia on schedule. We'll have to give up Orvieto and substitute another spot. How about Assisi?"

I laughed.

"What's funny?"

"Nothing really. Assisi would be great."

A few hours later, she had things rearranged.

"No room in the inn," Austen said. "Assisi's booked. Something's going on there. I've reserved a room in Bevagna, a small town about 10 miles from Assisi. I think you'll like it. You can drive to Assisi and spend the day there if you like."

Two days later, I landed in Rome and drove to Bevagna. It was a quiet place—very quiet. There were a few tourists, but mostly it was locals living their lives in an unpretentious, picturesque spot well off the beaten path. For early October, it was still quite warm. My hotel sat just outside the town's impressive wall. I unpacked and wandered into town, shaking off a nagging case of jet lag. As I passed what looked like an old monastery, I felt a sudden rush of energy.

"We were here," Grace said.

"We?"

"Yes," she said. "You know. Trust your remembering."

"Clare?" I asked. "St. Clare?"

There was laughter and clapping from somewhere inside the old building.

"That's the connection I just felt. You were here? I was here?"

"Yes and now you're back. Connecting to the old, planting the new."

"Doing what?"

"You've connected to your earthly life as Francis to support the energy you carry. At the same time, with each step, you anchor new energy in this place—the energy of awakening. You receive and you give what's needed. You'll remember more in time."

"Nice to get a straight answer for a change."

"Easy," M said.

"So, are you Grace or Clare?"

"You call me Grace. I like that. I was Clare in my life with you as Francis, but Grace is nice."

The next day I drove to Assisi right after breakfast to beat the traffic and the heat.

I beat neither.

Parking lots near town were full. Parking lots a long way from town were full. Bus parking lots were full. Everything was full. People swarmed like ants up a long, winding road to the walled town center at the top of a high hill. The enormous Basilica of St. Francis sat atop the hill. The not-quite-so-enormous Basilica of St. Clare anchored the other end of town. Both were a long way from where I stood.

I could have walked from Bevagna, I thought. The stress of crowds and heat were already getting to me.

"You've walked these hills many times," Grace said. "Calmly. Enjoying the warm sunshine."

"Okay. I deserved that. Is it always like this?"

"Patience," she said.

"Not my strong suit. I don't walk willingly into crowds."

"I know."

Like the rest of the madding crowd, I hiked uphill to a great plaza in front of St. Francis' Basilica. It was jam-packed with people, television trucks, satellite dishes, and all-too-visible, heavily-armed soldiers. A very long, loosely defined line snaked its way to the basilica's front doors.

Oh, bother, I thought, searching for the end of the line.

I hate standing in line.

A couple from Boston were in front of me. I asked what was going on.

"It's the Feast Day of St. Francis."

"I had no idea it was anybody's feast day. What are they serving?"

"Quite the party, huh?"

"Leave it to me to pick the busiest day of the year."

As I waited in line outside the basilica, Grace said, "This is where it happens. Not in there. Out here." I felt a wave of energy.

Inside, thousands of people sitting in pews and standing in the aisles faced the altar which seemed a football field distant. Solemn priests in bright white robes and very tall, pointed hats lined the altar facing us and spoke in Latin. I could barely hear them but it didn't matter. My Latin's not all that great.

"This is not where it happens," Grace said.

The line wound its way through the suffocating crowd to well-worn stone steps. It looked like we were heading to the basement.

"Where are we going?" I whispered to the lady in front of me, pointing down the steps.

"The crypt," she whispered.

Crypt?

At the bottom of the steps, I stood in front of St. Francis' tomb. Like everybody else there, I watched flames flicker on a row of candles in front of the tomb for a moment and moved along.

"What do you feel?" Grace asked.

"Nothing," I said.

"This is not where it happens," she said.

Back outside in the crowded plaza, Grace was quick to say, "This is where it happens."

Without a destination in mind, I walked away from the crowd looking for a quieter spot, and after wandering several narrow cobblestone streets, I found one—a small coffee shop. I sat for a few minutes in the garden behind the shop sipping a cappuccino.

When I stepped back into the street, Grace said, "Let's walk down the hill."

As I walked, the crowds thinned to near nothing. The street led to another large plaza outside the Basilica of St. Clare—smaller and less imposing than Francis' place but still huge. There was no feast, so no trucks, satellite dishes or armed guards. A few people sat on a stone wall in the shade. It was delightfully peaceful.

I walked into the cavernous nave and wandered around for a while.

"This is not where it happens," Grace said.

St. Clare's remains were on view in a glass case in the crypt below the basilica's altar. I stood looking at her skeleton wondering why anybody'd want to see it.

"I'm way better looking than that," Grace said.

"I know," I said aloud, forgetting where I was.

They guy next to me turned and shushed me with a finger to his lips.

Back outside, Grace said again, "This is where it happens."

"Okay, I'm glad I came but it's time to get out of here before church lets out up the hill. I don't want to get stuck in that crowd."

"A little shopping before you leave?" Grace asked. "You've got time. Something for your cottage?"

"I'm not much of a shopper…"

I felt a nudge of energy as I walked by a small gift shop. The door was open.

"Just a quick look around," Grace said.

I stepped inside, out of the intense sunshine. I glanced at a painted tile on a shelf to my left.

"For the cottage," Grace said, and I felt another wave of energy.

I took a closer look—Francis cutting Clare's long, beautiful hair, as she joined Francis and his followers.

"That's you," Grace said. "We had a beautiful partnership. Don't forget who you are. Never forget who you are."

The tile now stands propped against the wall on a shelf in the cottage. I see it almost every day. It reminds me who I am.

Mona Lisa

A DAY OR two after my trip to Italy, M said. "You'll start painting soon."

"Painting? Are you kidding?"

"Not kidding."

"If that happens, no one will be more surprised than me, but an awful lot of folks will be equally surprised."

There were some things I knew about myself—fundamental truths mostly learned the hard way over the better part of a lifetime.

One of the things I knew was this: I produced my best artwork in kindergarten. It was good enough to be taped to the refrigerator door for a day, maybe two, before disappearing to goodness knows where. My artistic predilections, if I had any, tumbled downhill from there.

At one point I asked Coco if she'd kept a file of my artwork. Maybe she had some of it squirreled away in a closet. She'd kept most everything else.

"I doubt it," she said.

When your own mother thinks your artwork stinks, there's a strong message there somewhere.

A couple of months later, on a cold, dreary January day, I sat in the cottage without much to do. I'd finished reading a book and was glad to be done with it. Friends were busy elsewhere, so I'd planned a nice long walk by myself that included a stop for lunch, but my plan wasn't going to happen. When it's too dreary to walk, it's exceedingly dreary. I don't lean toward depression, but if ever there were a day to retreat to a darkened bedroom, this was it.

"Your painting," M said. "Would this be a good day to start painting?"

"I thought you'd let that go. What do you not understand about my artistic abilities?"

"A belief," she said. "All your beliefs are too small. Like boxes, they imprison you. Let them go. They're in your way."

"Well, that particular belief has a solid foundation in history."

"Those are the beliefs that are most in your way. Let them go."

Well, okay. I had nothing else to do. What was the worst that could happen? I warmed to the idea. Maybe a few tubes of paint would provide a nice diversion. I had an empty spot in the cottage where I could make a mess without disturbing much.

The sales guy at the art store didn't know what to do with me.

"Think of me as a blank canvas," I said. "It's actually worse than that, but you don't want to hear it."

An hour later I had oil paints, solvent, brushes, several canvases (the cheap ones), a painter's drop cloth, and an easel. The sales guy grinned as he punched keys on the cash register.

"Have fun," he said. "Call if you have questions."

"If I never see you again, you'll know you helped me confirm what I already know. I can't reliably draw a stick figure."

"You'll be back," he said.

I set up the easel and dropped the drop cloth. I put my paints and brushes on the table by the cottage sink and stepped back. It all looked artistic and slightly promising.

Hmmm, I thought. *This'll be interesting. All we need now is an artist.*

"We have one," M said.

I heard laughter and clapping from somewhere in the cottage loft.

"Living is creating. Every thought, every feeling, every movement, and every moment between," M said. "Your paintings will help you. Like your dreams, they'll help you remember who you are and point the way."

As you might guess, my early attempts at painting were awkward. I opened coffee table books and tried to paint the beautiful pictures I found there. My paintings didn't look much like the pictures. So I looked out the window and tried to paint what I saw. My paintings didn't look much like what I saw. Even so, painting was strangely enjoyable. There was something drawing me forward. I kept going.

I experimented with colors and brushes. I painted over, left messy globs of paint where they lay, and used solvent to rub out spots that didn't look quite right to me. In short, I played. I quit trying to paint anything in particular and simply played. And it started to flow. The canvases began to reveal themselves. I'd see what wanted to be there and work with it. I soon gave up the brushes and used my fingers or old rags instead. I liked the feel of the canvas and the smell of the paint. At some point I'd step back and look at what was there. And I loved what I saw. And I learned to let it be. Whether or not anyone else appreciated my painting, I loved it.

"What is it?" Caroline asked, looking at one of my early masterpieces.

"I don't know," I said.

"Interesting," she said.

I heard the word *interesting* a lot.

Soon I felt energy at my fingertips when I touched a canvas and the experience of painting became surreal.

"Your paintings carry your energy," M said. "It touches those who're open to it. You're remembering how to play—allowing your creativity to move through you onto the canvas. Creativity is part of who you are. Nurture it as you nurture your garden. Be patient and watch your canvases produce great beauty for you." She laughed, "Whether others appreciate it or not."

"Interesting," my daughters said.

"Interesting," friends said.

"Interesting," the electrician said.

Over time, themes emerged. There were lots of winding roads going up hills past lone trees. (Your path, I heard.) There were horizons. (No boundaries, I heard.) There were lone circles and then intersecting circles. (Moving to wholeness I heard.) There were natural disasters— typhoons, forest fires, animals staring at me from the canvas. (The Earth cries out to you, I heard.) There were portraits of folks I didn't know. (You do know, I heard.) There were scenes from events I didn't know. (You do know, I heard.)

I never knew what a canvas wanted to be when I stepped up to it, but I learned to place my fingers on the canvas and let go. What emerged simply emerged. The less I tried, the better things went.

Wow, I thought. *I love this.*

During the fall of 2015, I went through a challenging few months. That's a story for another time. It suffices to say, I was offered the opportunity to work with a great deal of sadness and regret only to discover there was nothing to be sad about or regret. Those few months were, in retrospect, full of beauty, but it was hard to see as I walked through it. I endured some dismal days.

"We need to lighten you up," M said.

"Good luck. The joy of living escapes me at the moment."

"Want to play? Paint something?"

"Not really."

"I'll help you. It'll be fun," M said. "And you'll remember something we enjoyed together in that other life. Something that connected us."

"Connected us?"

I went out to the cottage and put a new canvas on the easel. I picked up an old rag.

"Use your hands, just your fingers. They'll help you remember. And mix a light pink for color. Put your fingers on the canvas. I'll guide you."

And she did.

"Lighter pink there. A little darker there for shadow. A bit of red there. Round the edge there. And on the other side…"

So it went for an hour or so. I had no idea what I was painting.

"A flower?" I asked.

"Remember," M said.

"I don't know…" I started.

"You do know," M said. "Step back and see."

I stepped back from the canvas.

"An orchid blossom?"

The cottage was very quiet. I felt anticipation in the air, like lots of folks were holding their breath. Waiting…

"A vagina?" I said.

The cottage burst with laughter.

"We had a lot of fun with that flower," M said. "Remember?"

" I don't, but I wish I did."

"Over time, maybe the painting will help you remember."

"I hope so."

"Feeling a little better?" M asked.

"Much," I said.

⇥⬤ ⬤⇤

Painting is a part of my new normal—one of my favorite ways to pass time. It reminds me of things and often points the way. I haven't painted the Mona Lisa yet. People still look at my paintings and, not knowing what else to say, mouth the word *interesting*.

"Life is like your painting," M said. "Things go best when you stop trying to make something and allow yourself to discover what life wants to be. Allow it to come to you."

End Game

THE VILLAGE OF Chinley nestles in a small valley on the edge of England's Peak District National Park. It's surrounded by great bald hills, perfect for day-hiking within sight of dinner and a comfortable bed. It was exactly what I wanted.

I stayed in a cottage at Old Hall Inn. The cottage was a short walk from the main hotel and restaurant. Each day, I ate a leisurely breakfast in front of a warm fire before pulling on my hiking boots and shouldering my daypack. An hour later, out of breath after a steep climb, I stood high atop the world buffeted by brisk winds and spitting rain. I walked the hilltops alone with my thoughts for several hours before returning to the cottage for a shower and a pre-dinner nap. There weren't a lot of dinner alternatives in the village and that was okay because the Inn's food was hearty, delicious and sleep-inducing. After dinner, I pretended to read for a while before nodding off, only to rise the next morning and do it all over again. I'd gladly go back. Maybe one of these days, I will.

For the first few days, my time was my own—no voices, no visions, no remembering, no energetic adjustments. If I dreamed, I wasn't aware of it. I enjoyed the quiet until loneliness crept in late in the afternoon on the third day. As I walked a wind-swept path through a herd of sheep grazing in a shallow dip between hills, lambs bounded all around me. Even the lambs couldn't cheer me up.

"Yours is a solitary path," M said. "You walk alone but are never alone."

"Thank you," I said. "I'm grateful, but right now…"

"We know. Be patient. This will pass. Look to the horizon, across the tops of the hills. See what lies beyond. Much is unfolding for you. Allow it to come to you."

That night I slept and dreamed…

I sat on an old stone bridge abutment high above a river flowing silently far below. I could see the other abutment, or what had once been an abutment, across the river. It was a decrepit pile of stones. The bridge that once crossed the river was long gone.

The river ran crystal clear. I could easily see the rocky bottom and watched fish feeding in the meandering current. Over time the river had carved itself into a steep-sided, forested gorge. Sitting quietly on the crumbling abutment under a clear blue sky, I heard birds singing in the trees around me. There were no people and, other than the aging bridge abutments, no evidence human beings had ever been there.

It was a memorable place—peaceful, spacious, eternal.

I woke up.

Lying in bed, I replayed the dream in my head—so vivid and inviting. I wanted to go back.

"You will," M said.

The next morning, sturdy English umbrella in hand, I walked to breakfast in driving rain. The sky was ominously dark. The surrounding hilltops appeared and disappeared in fast moving clouds swirling around them.

Maybe I'll do a little reading this morning. I thought. *Have a cup of tea.*

While I loved the walking, part of me was glad to have a rest day. After breakfast, I went back to the cottage, put a kettle on the stove, built a fire in the tiny fireplace, played some quiet music on my phone, and settled on the sofa, listening to rain pelting the roof.

Without warning, the top of my head began to tingle and energy flowed through me. A new voice began speaking slowly but clearly. It was a man's voice.

"You are *the healer*," he said, with effort. "You've come back in this life to spread a *new energy* across the Earth. The new energy, created by your Father and delivered through you, facilitates *apotheosis*—opening you and your brethren to their divinity. The energy comes with a *plenitude of your Father's grace*.

"The energy is powerful and beyond the physical ability of one human personality. You join with other personalities in your soul family at this time to facilitate the energy's flow. You have connected with two of these personalities. You soon connect with others. Be patient and allow these connections as they come to you. Your understanding will grow as the connections are made.

"We are a group of beings on other planes of existence *gathered* to support this evolution in human consciousness. We are legion. We are the Gathering. We are with you. Always with you.

"Apotheosis is a challenging process, offering you the opportunity to face fear and *remember* there's nothing to fear. Stepping through fear, you see the world differently. Old ways of seeing, believing and doing lose their attraction. New ways take their places. You step into your autonomy. No one stands between you and your Creator. Only love remains. You love yourself, others, the Earth, and all her creatures. You love All There Is.

"This evolution in human consciousness is what many call the *apocalypse*. As so many of you step into and through fear, a great swirl of human emotions will erupt. Like all things, this too will pass in time.

"In your dream, you saw beyond the apocalypse—a thousand years into the future. In that time, as you experienced it, the Earth is healthy. There are many fewer humans on the Earth. That's why you didn't see other people or much evidence of them—just the crumbling abutments.

The humans who inhabit the Earth in that time are caretakers, not destroyers.

"In this way, humankind realizes its fullest expression in love and creativity.

"You are the healer. Never forget who you are."

Suddenly the room was still—very still. It was a few minutes before I noticed the Beatles' song *Blackbird* playing on my phone and heard these words,

You were only waiting for this moment to arise.

Energy moved through me in great waves. The room filled with joy. I felt the joy, along with a sobering dose of fear—my nagging fear of not being good enough.

"Enjoy the moment," M said. "Let go of fear and step through. You've seen the future in your dream—far beyond the next hill. You now know. Trust your knowing."

⊷▬◉ ◉▬⊶

A couple of days later I joined a friend and his son for a walking trip in the Yorkshire Dales. We started in Ilkley, walking along the River Wharfe to Grassington where we planned to spend the night. My friend's son took the lead, leaving his dad and me strolling at a more leisurely pace far behind. As we walked, I told my friend about my experience in Chinley and seeing a thousand years into the future in my dream.

At Barden, a literal bump in the road, our walk crossed the River Wharfe via Barden Bridge. As I walked across the bridge and looked down at the river below, I knew. I was walking across the bridge that wouldn't be there a thousand years hence. I was there.

Energy poured through me as it had after the revelations of Chinley.

"This is it," I said to my friend. "The bridge. The one in my dream. I dreamed about sitting on that abutment there, next to where you're standing, and now we're here. Mary Magdalene said I'd see this again and here we are. I can't make this stuff up."

"Extraordinary," my friend said, looking back across the bridge. "Wow."

We stood at the shady end of the bridge for a while, watching the river's lazy flow. A fish fed in a thread of current along the river bank below. Birds sang in the treetop above us. And then we walked on.

Take a Cruise

BACK FROM MY walking trip, energy shifts came frequently. I often woke in the middle of the night, my body vibrating intensely head to toe. The vibrations continued for a couple of minutes and subsided before I fell asleep again.

In my dreams, a new theme showed itself:

It's nighttime. I'm on a boat dock. The light of a full moon shimmers on the water below the dock. I have a small skiff. I'm preparing it to motor across the ocean. I'm loading a gas can and connecting it to the skiff's outboard motor as an elderly white-haired gentleman in khakis and a tattered flannel shirt walks up the dock toward me. He's wearing a sailor's cap, smoking a pipe.

"Can I help you?" he asks. He looks familiar.

"I think I've got what I need, but thanks."

"Where you headed?"

"Across there," I say, pointing across the ocean.

"That's a big ocean. You'll run into some powerful storms. Sure you have what you need?"

"I have a life vest," I answered, tilting the boat motor into place.

The old guy smiled at me, sucked on his pipe and blew smoke into the air.

"Think I should carry a spare can of gas?"

He chuckled and pointed out to sea with the stem of his pipe.

"Son, if you're planning to cross *that* ocean, you'll need a lot more than a skiff and a spare can of gas. You're going to need a bigger boat. Better wait till you get a bigger boat."

I woke up.

"What was that about?" M asked.

"Who knows?" I said, still groggy with sleep. "Let's make this easy. You tell me."

"Surely you know by now that's not likely to happen," she said. "I think you know what that was about."

I thought for a minute.

"The way ahead is longer and more challenging than I'm prepared to handle now. My boat's not big enough to make the trip. A life vest and another can of gas won't do it. I'm getting a bigger boat. The energy adjustments. Need to wait till I have a bigger boat."

"Nice," M said. "Patience is needed now. You enter a period of additional adjustments. This will happen slowly as you see things. You're getting a bigger boat. One that'll carry you across the ocean and over some big waves. You're being prepared to move through the swirl."

"Swirl?"

"You're a disruptive force. Remember? Sorry to repeat myself, but this is important. It's part of who you are. You turn things upside down. You'll frighten people—challenging their ways of believing, seeing and doing. Their fear is their opening. If they're willing to face their fear and walk through the opening, your Father's grace will see them through. But many will avoid stepping into their fear. Some will be stuck, unable to move. Some will try to retreat to their comfortable lives. It won't work, but they'll try. Others will choose to fight. They'll try to stop you. This won't work either, but they'll try. This is the swirl. You've walked through the swirl many times. You'll walk through it again, but this time you must be prepared to weather a much bigger storm and the enormous waves it will bring. This is your path."

"Did I sign up for this? I don't remember signing up for this. Surely I didn't sign up for this. I think you have the wrong guy."

M laughed. "You said *yes* to this long before you came back to Earth. You wouldn't be here otherwise. We have the right guy. Remember who you are. You're the healer."

M paused to let that sink in, then continued.

"There's someone here for you."

"Someone new?"

"Not new," M said. "She's always with you—just stepping forward. She was your mother in another life. She likes lettuce and tomato on a turkey sandwich."

I remembered my dream.

"The older woman in the blue dress?"

"Exactly," M said.

"Mary. Mother Mary."

"Yes," M said. "She's here. Always with you. Watching over you. She holds a white rose for you. She hopes you'll never tire of healing. She sends you much love."

I felt a beautiful energy move through me.

"One more thing," M said.

"More? What more could you possibly have to say?"

M laughed. "Have you forgotten who I am?"

Little Man

NIGHTTIME—ROUGHLY 3 TO 4 o'clock in the morning—was class time. Almost every night, I woke up in the middle of a dream or energy shift. For the next hour or so, I'd talk with M or Sarah or Grace about what was happening—whatever it was. I called these sessions *tutorials* when I mentioned them to the few close friends who were familiar with my story, but I was reminded that I wasn't learning anything. I was simply remembering what I already knew.

"Right," I said. "But it feels like elementary school. You know how much I enjoyed elementary school."

"We'll try not to bore you," M said.

My bedroom was quiet. I looked at my alarm clock—yep, 3 o'clock in the morning—another tutorial right on schedule.

"So what's the lesson for tonight?" I asked.

"The savior gig is over," M said.

"What?"

"All those lives carrying the burden of salvation and so many opportunities along the way to lay the burden down. And now another opportunity presents itself. It's time to lay the burden down. It's not yours to carry."

"Good lord..." I started.

"Exactly," M said.

"Can we go back a step? What lives?"

"The two you've touched and others yet to show themselves."

"Jesus and Francis?"

"Yes, and others."

"You said burden of salvation. I carried the burden of salvation. What burden?"

"You've come to Earth many times, often to save the world through your words and deeds. You've shouldered the burden of fixing humankind by preaching and exemplary living, only to watch your fellow humans and their institutions twist your words and deeds to justify horrendous atrocities, lies and injustice—the unintended consequences of your lives. There has been good and a great deal of abuse. Many have been maimed and killed in your name. Your story—the story of the savior—no longer serves. It's time for a different story—the story of individual responsibility. It's time to lay your burden down, for yourself and your soul family and all of humankind. The savior gig is over."

"Goodness," I said.

I lay in bed for a minute or two, my mind churning.

"Okay. I know you're not done. Where do we go from here?"

"You have the opportunity to remember this now, for yourself and your soul family: *Sometimes helping isn't.*"

"Sometimes helping isn't? What…"

"Those of us who choose human lives come to face challenges, work with our fears, and take responsibility for our responses to them. It's the path to wholeness, freedom and love. When you take up someone else's challenge, you deprive him of the opportunity to do what he came to do, to move toward wholeness, to remember who he is, to touch his divinity. The savior deprives his fellow beings of personal responsibility. Sometimes what you see as helping, isn't helping at all."

"You say *sometimes* helping isn't…"

There are times when another can't carry his burden. In those times, it's appropriate to help, but only until he's able to take it up again. Knowing when to help is challenging. You're working with this now."

"I am?"

"You begin to notice that helping isn't working for you. You explore your motivations and see that much of what you call *helping* is often more for you than another. Let this come to you. You'll see and in seeing, you'll remember. And you'll lay your burden down. You'll be free. And in that place, you'll serve."

"Am I not here this time to save? You tell me I'm a healer. Is a healer different from a savior?"

"Nice," M said. "Allowing, not doing. Remember what Sarah told you?"

"Sarah's said a lot of things."

"God's got the pen."

Yes, she said that."

"Let this work in you now. See those words differently. Nothing to do. Allow the remembering to come to you."

And that's where M left it.

The clock said 4:17.

I couldn't sleep. I got out of bed and wandered around in the dark for a while before I made a cup of coffee and went out on the porch. A sliver of moon glowed over the neighborhood. All was quiet except for the grinding in my head. *The savior gig is over.*

⋆⇒ ⇐⋆

Since I first heard those words from M, I've had plenty of time to think about them and Sarah's words too, *God got da pen.* I understand now that *being* a healer is different from *doing* the work of a savior. No trying to save anybody. No trying to heal anybody. Only exercising my personal responsibility and allowing God's healing to flow through me. *God got da pen.*

I'm privileged to know the purpose of this life, but I need not carry the full weight of it—only my small part. *God got da pen.*

It's easy for me to write these words. Living them is more challenging. Laying down the savior's burden is hard for me. One day, after noticing yet another opportunity to resist *helping,* I found myself stepping in to help where helping wasn't.

Good lord, I thought. *I can't do this by myself. I need help.*

"Nice," M said.

That night I dreamed this dream:

I'm in the house I called home as a child. In the kitchen. It's nighttime. There aren't any lights on. It's dark but I can see well enough to find my way. Someone is there. A boy, I think. A young boy.

I feel a wave of pleasant energy.

I can't see him, but I know he's there.

"Who are you?" I ask, but there's no response.

I glimpse him walking down the hall toward my bedroom. I follow in the dark. At the door to my bedroom, I reach to flip the light switch, but I have no hands. I have no body.

I can't flip a light switch without a body, I think.

Frustrated, I speak into the dark room, "Who are you?"

There's still no response.

The whole scene suddenly feels ominous.

I turn to leave but stop myself.

I can't run. I have to see who's here. Find out what this is about.

Instantly a lamp lights my bedroom.

Interesting, I think.

I walk in and look around. I don't see the boy.

"Where are you?"

Again, no response.

I look in the closet, the bathroom and under one of the twin beds. No one there.

I get down on the floor to look under the other bed. There he is. Lying on his back. Barefoot. Wearing jeans and a white t-shirt. He's young, maybe 8 or 9 years old. I tap him on the shoulder.

"Who are you? Why are you hiding?"

No response.

He rolls out from under the bed on the other side and leaves the room. I get up to follow. He walks down the hall, through the kitchen and out the door into the backyard.

Standing in the backyard, I don't see him. There's enough of a moon to see my shadow on the ground. I don't have a body but I have a shadow.

Strange, I think.

I'm suddenly aware that I'm in a dream and can go wherever I like. I feel the boy's energy. He's hiding. He's scared. *Of what?* I wonder.

I feel another wave of encouraging energy.

And then I know I'm the boy. I'm climbing the old sycamore tree in the neighbor's backyard. I reach the upper branches, sit down on a sturdy limb and lean back against the tree trunk. I look out on the old neighborhood, bathed in moonlight. All is quiet and peaceful. I relax, seeing the houses, yards, the hill across the street, the tree I planted long ago, the tree house, the old swing set. And I remember.

Another sprinkling of energy.

This tree was my refuge. This is where I came to get away. This old tree held me—strong, safe, quiet—where nobody could find me. I was safe. I could relax.

I woke up and the memories came flooding back.

"What you rememberin', child?" Sarah asked.

"I'm not…"

"You was 8. Jus' a lil' fella. What you rememberin'?"

"I was scared."

"O' what?"

"I was afraid I couldn't hold it together."

"What you tryin' to hold?"

"My family. I remember yelling. My parents yelling at each other. My little brothers and me, we were scared. Coco telling me I had to help her. Take care of my brothers. Help her hold it together. Dad was a doctor and mostly gone. She told me I was the man of the house and I had to help her hold it together.

"When my dad was home, there was tension and sometimes yelling. I'd close my door waiting for the yelling to stop. But it didn't stop till I went and told them to stop. I was so scared. I feel it now. So afraid it was all going to blow apart. Where would I take my brothers? Where would we live? Who would help us? Would the neighbors keep us? How would I let my aunt know? I didn't know how to call her. Would the neighbors help me call her? Would she come help us?

"I was scared but I couldn't show it. Be the strong one, Coco said. I need you to be the strong one. Be a good example for your brothers. They look up to you.

"I tried so hard.

"And I never told anyone. I was too scared...

"Sometimes I'd run out the back door to the tree and climb up where nobody could see me and sit until the terror went away...I couldn't..."

And then I lost it. I lay in bed, weeping. I couldn't talk through the tears.

"I was so afraid..."

"Quiet now, child. Let da tears do they job. Let 'em go. So much you been holdin'. Tryin' to hold together fo' yo'self and everbody else. Savin' yo'self and everbody else. Keepin' everbody safe. Bein' strong. A lifetime of savin'. Now time for lettin' go. Dat savior gig's over. It done. God got da pen. You free, child. You ever more free."

Do It Yourself

I LAY ON Bonnie's table, receiving yet more healing.

"You quite da projec'," Sarah said.

At the end of our session, Bonnie left the room briefly and returned with a small, badly tarnished silver container, about the diameter of a quarter. It had a screw top.

"I was asked to give you this. They say you'll know what to do."

"What is it?"

"It's called an oil stock, I think. It holds anointing oil. I bought it years ago. I don't remember why. It's been in my desk drawer since. It used to have oil in it. It's probably rancid now. I tried to unscrew the top but couldn't. Maybe you can get the top off."

I couldn't unscrew the top either.

"Anointing oil? What do I do with it?"

"I don't know," Bonnie said. "I was asked to give it to you. I'm curious too. Let me know when you figure it out. Maybe WD-40 will help. The top's probably rusted shut."

I put the little container in my pocket and went home.

"What's this for?" I asked.

"Put it in the cottage, on a shelf. You'll know when it's needed," M said.

"Am I going to anoint somebody?"

"Yes," M said.

"Who?"

No answer.

I tried again to unscrew the cap, but couldn't. The cap was stuck. I put the oil stock in the cottage and soon forgot about it.

Sometime thereafter, I lay on Sandy's table while she manipulated my jaw.

"There's someone new here."

"I feel something… but don't know…what do you see?"

"He's old. Really old. Wrinkled. He looks ancient. He looks serious."

"Who is he?"

"I'm asking," Sandy said. "It takes a lot of energy for him to speak. He speaks slowly, with effort. *Serov*? It's a long name. I hear *Serov* but there's more. He says *Serov* will do. Call him *Serov*."

"I know him," I say. "Not the name, but I know him. Somehow I know him. He directs the Gathering. He spoke to me in Chinley, when I was in England on the walking trip."

"Yes," Sandy said. "He's nodding slowly. He moves slowly."

"I don't know how I know him. I don't remember…"

He says …" Sandy started.

"It's time," I said. "Yes I hear him. It's time. Time for what?"

"You know," Sandy said. "He's nodding."

"Maybe so, but it's not coming to me. Can he tell us?"

"He's smiling and now he goes away."

"Well, at least that part's familiar."

"There are so many here," Sandy said. "All around. Mother Mary, Mary Magdalene, Francis, Sarah, Grace, Jesus…so many…and a choir…singing …from books…in robes…this is holy…a holy time… oh Steve, I've never seen such a thing…a host of holies, they say…the Gathering…"

"I feel them. Like the class at Bonnie's. It feels the same…"

"It is," Sandy said. "I don't know what they say now. Do you have something small? Silver? Some oil?"

"Bonnie gave me an oil stock."

"Yes," Sandy said. "That's it. It's time. You know, they say."

"Oh brother."

"Everybody's very happy, Steve. It's time."

Several days later, M asked me to retrieve the oil stock from the cottage and put oil in it. Olive oil and a few drops of frankincense. I went to the cottage, picked up the oil stock and held it in my hand. I still couldn't twist the top off. *Wonder what this is about?*

Bonnie told me the oil stock contained anointing oil. I had only a vague idea about anointing. Putting oil on a person's head? Like baptism but with oil? I didn't really know what the word meant, so I looked it up. *To smear or rub with oil, to apply oil as part of a religious ceremony, to choose by divine election.*

I tried the top again. This time it twisted off easily.

"It's time," M said.

A discolored piece of dry cotton was inside. I tossed the piece of cotton and washed the stock.

"Another bit of cotton, some olive oil and a couple of drops of frankincense," M suggested.

" I have everything but the frankincense. I'll have to order some."

"In the pantry," M said.

Years ago, I bought some essential oils because a friend from the Brazil trip sold them as part of her business. She suggested a selection of oils and I bought them and put them on a shelf in the kitchen pantry. They'd been there a long time. Sure enough, I found the frankincense and prepared the oil stock.

"You can put it back on the shelf in the cottage. Let it rest there."

"When do I anoint somebody?"

"Soon," M said. "You'll know."

Early Christmas morning, the cottage garden was white with a dusting of snow. The neighborhood was quiet.

I felt a shower of energy.

"Merry Christmas," M said. "It's time."

"For what?"

"The anointing."

"But there's nobody here."

"You're here."

"Well, sure, but…"

"Would you like to go out to the cottage?"

It was more instruction than query. I've been known to bristle at instruction.

"You've always bristled at instruction. It's part of who you are. There's wisdom in your response to instruction."

I went to the cottage with my cup of coffee, Yoda trundling along behind. Inside, he circled a spot on the rug several times before sitting down and staring disapprovingly at me. Yoda likes his morning routine. We never go to the cottage before breakfast. As far as he was concerned, we were off-road. Where was his breakfast?

M didn't seem concerned about Yoda. "The oil stock," she said.

I picked it up and unscrewed the top.

Energy electrified every part of me. It came in waves and continued without slowing.

"Dip your finger into the stock and rub a bit of the oil on your forehead."

"I'm supposed to anoint myself? Don't we need a priest or something?"

Serov stepped forward, speaking slowly. "Who do you deem worthy to stand between you and your Father? Who better than you to anoint you?"

He had a point.

"And why am I doing this?"

"You are chosen," he said. "You are the healer."

Goodness, I thought.

"Welcome back," M said.

"We's lovin' you, child. Merry Christmas," Sarah said. "You bringin' yo' gift to da world."

The energy came in powerful waves as I dabbed a few drops of oil on my forehead.

"It's done," Serov said.

I heard a choir singing. The cottage filled with joy. I don't know another way to describe the feeling of it—pure joy like what I felt in Chinley.

As the energy subsided and the singing faded, Yoda got up.

"Arooooooo," he said.

"Okay. Okay," I said. "I guess we're done here. How about a special Christmas breakfast for you? Your favorite dog food and a short walk?"

"Arooooooo," he said, trundling toward the door. You could tell he didn't care much for anointings.

⇥ ⇤

A week or two later, I was back at Sandy's. She was fiddling with my jaw.

"There's somebody here for you," she said, stepping back from my head.

"Serov?"

"He's here, but there's somebody else. He's standing at your head, between us now."

"I feel him."

"He's wearing a white linen robe and a light blue shawl. *The robe,* he says. Do you know who this is?"

Somehow I did know.

"It's me," I said. "My soul."

"Ooooh, I got chicken skin," Sandy said. (It's her Swiss translation of goose bumps.)

"Me too," I said. "I hear it's time to wear the robe."

"Yes. Oh, Steve, so beautiful. He places his hands lightly on your head. Time to wear the robe. Serov is nodding. What does it mean?"

"I don't know," I said.

Wear the Robe

Wear the robe?

You'd think I might have gotten a little more guidance than that, but no. I felt myself opening to a bit of instruction if it'd help me understand what wearing the robe meant.

The only additional thing Serov had to say was "Getting smarter slowly."

That sparked boisterous laughter among the Gathering.

Singularly unhelpful, I thought.

I was left alone to wonder about wearing the robe. I knew the robe was white with a light blue shawl. The idea was inviting. A robe sounded comfortable, but not terribly fashionable—at least, not in Nashville. Maybe Serov wasn't suggesting a literal robe. Perhaps the whole idea was metaphorical or maybe he was suggesting I shop for some new loose-fitting clothes—like a pair of white linen pants, a breezy blue island shirt, and flip flops. I could get into that. And I could grow my hair out, let the beard fill out a bit, and get a tasteful New Age doodad of some sort to hang on a hemp necklace around my neck. That sounded cool. I'd move to Hawaii. That also sounded cool. Or Bali. That sounded cooler.

Finally I had some direction. A plan was taking shape in my head. I'd have to write it down—make a list. I was back on track. Doing what I do best. I was a go-getter again.

And then shit—a lot of it—hit the fan. A friend fell into deep depression. (He was suicidal for months.) There were business snafus.

(I'm pretty much retired. I thought I was done with that stuff.) There were house repairs—lots of them. (I'd already spent a bundle on the place.) Yoda was sick, throwing up everything he ate. (He's an old dog, the vet said.) There were relationship issues. (Shared experience showed its dark side.) A family of rabbits moved into the garden and commenced gnawing on the Hostas. (I love my Hostas.)

Challenges abounded. There were days when I felt like I was watching a soap opera happening on my side of the TV screen. I forgot about the robe and Bali.

"Step forward slowly," Serov said.

"Aware, not afraid," M said.

"Movin' to da easy place," Sarah said.

"Easy? You're calling this easy?"

I thought seriously about escaping to a kinder, gentler place. If not Bali, maybe I'd move back to Seattle. I could move back if I wanted and ditch this mess. My mind wandered down that track one afternoon as I drove to get the oil changed in my car. Simple, right? What could possibly go wrong?

"We'll have your car back to you in half an hour," Clint said. "Have a seat in our waiting area and get yourself a cup of coffee. I'll let you know when the car's ready."

I sat on a sofa. There were several other customers waiting—poking at cell phones, staring at computer screens, and rummaging through purses. I looked at the magazines on the coffee table in front of me. A tired-looking National Geographic lay on top of the pile. The cover featured a picture of Pope Francis.

I felt a tingling of energy.

I reached to pick up the magazine, but thought better of it. Lots of people had put their hands on it. Colds were going around. *Germs*, I thought. *Probably lots of germs.*

I sat and twiddled my thumbs. I could have checked my phone but there was little point. The cold shoulder of pesky relationship challenges left me message-less.

"Mr. Johnson, your car's ready," Clint said.

"Great. That was quick. Thanks."

I paid for the oil change and got in my car. Clint smiled and waved goodbye. I turned the key and nothing happened—nothing.

Clint frowned.

"I'll have it checked out. Can't imagine what's happened. I drove it in here. No problem. And now…"

"I'll go back and sit on the sofa," I said. Compared to what was happening in the rest of my life, sitting on the sofa at the oil change place was nice.

I sat again staring at the Pope's picture. I reached for the magazine, but thought better of it.

About half an hour passed before Clint showed up. "Your car's ready. We couldn't find anything wrong. Don't know what that was about. But it's fine now."

I got in my car. Clint smiled and waved goodbye. I turned the key and nothing happened—nothing.

Clint frowned again.

"Let me try," Clint said. He turned the key and nothing happened. "I'm so sorry…"

"I'll go back and sit on the sofa," I said. I was actually looking forward to it.

Once again, I sat staring at the Pope's picture. This time I picked up the magazine, flipped pages till I found the article, and started reading. *I'll wash my hands before I leave,* I thought.

The article was about Pope Francis and his new job. Early on, one of his assistants told him he'd have to wear a bullet-proof vest when he went out in public. Pope Francis waved him off. He said something like *The Lord has placed me here for a purpose. He'll have to watch over me.*

My body vibrated head to toe when I read those words.

"Nothing to fear," M said. "You step through challenges now to remember who you are—your presence. Standing peacefully in the midst of the swirl. You've done this many times before. It's what you've taught. It's what you've lived. It's who you are."

"Wearin' da robe, child. Dat wearin' da robe," Sarah added.

Right on cue, Clint returned with my keys.

"Mr. Johnson, your car's ready. We replaced the battery cables and checked everything again. Nothing to pay. Sorry for your trouble. Have a nice evening."

"No problem," I said. "Thank you."

I got in my car. Clint smiled and waved goodbye. I turned the key and drove away.

I'm glad I finally read that article. I'd still be sitting on that sofa if I hadn't. *The Lord has placed me here for a purpose. He'll have to watch over me.*

While I'm not begging for another spate of disasters, I appreciate the ones I had. I'm a bit more trusting, a bit less afraid, a bit more loving, and a little better at standing peacefully in the swirl. That's wearing the robe.

So much for the linen pants, breezy shirt and Bali. It all sounded so nice....

Walk Alone

ONE DAY SEROV showed up looking much younger, even dapper.

He said slowly, " You'll walk alone for a while."

I'd heard similar things from M and others. I didn't ask questions. I wondered what he meant and why he was saying it then, but I'd find out soon enough. By now, I was practiced in the art of hearing words from the beyond and building mental stories around them. Some of the stories were quite good if I do say so myself. In time, I learned there was something I could count on: none of my stories were true. I could waste time making them up in my head or simply wait to see what happened. Waiting was, and still is, a lot easier.

I love to walk and I'm happy to walk alone most of the time.

"Part of who you are," M said. "You have a long history of walking alone. But you never walk alone."

"Follow yo' heart, child. You rememberin' how," Sarah said. "Let yo' heart lead."

So I did. I heard a song—Take Me Back to Chicago—got a rush of energy and booked a flight. Somebody mentioned a Five Rhythms dance class. Sounded interesting. I got an energy nudge and danced. I saw a poster for an art show, got a tingle, and went. I got a lot of energy-laced prodding and was, for the first time in my life, sort of spontaneous. I walked in New York, Chicago, the Florida Panhandle, the mountains of North Carolina, Seattle, Maui, and Montana—city streets, museums, urban parks, beaches, river walks, and mountain trails.

And the energy flowed. Oh, how it flowed. The more I followed my heart, the better it flowed—powerful, smooth and easy.

"In joy," Sarah said. "En-joy. Enjoy. Yo' heart know. Followin' yo' heart. Beautiful, child. We all in joy fo' you. You findin' da way. Da easy place. Who you is. You free. You ever more free."

"Your walking prepares you for what comes," M said. "You connect to other lives now. They come forward to support you. You uncover more of who you are. Step forward, always following your heart."

Ground Zero

I LANDED IN Tel Aviv. As the plane taxied to the gate, energy flowed through me powerfully.

"Welcome back," M said.

It was early March. The sun was hot, but nicely tempered by a constant sea breeze. Tel Aviv surprised me. It's a vibrant, aggressively modernizing city where two-story cinder block buildings sit uncomfortably in the lengthening shadows of steel and glass. It looked like a nice place to do some walking—alone.

I walked along the beach and explored back streets. I wandered through food markets and paid way too much for a small bag of figs. "Watch your pocket," the hotel manager told me. I ate some fabulous seafood and piping hot falafel. "Careful," the falafel guy said after I burned my tongue. As I walked, I acclimated to the place. I liked it.

After a couple of days in Tel Aviv, I hailed a taxi and headed to Jerusalem. My driver was ex-military. (I'd soon discover almost everybody was ex-military.) As we drove east into the hills, I saw crumbling villages on barren hillsides surrounded by impossibly tall chain-link fences topped with razor wire. They looked like prisons.

"Palestinian," my driver said.

There were other villages too— well-kept, no fences, no razor wire.

"Israeli," he said.

"So different from what I'd imagined. All I know is what I see on TV."

"The real West Bank," he said.

We topped a hill and there was Jerusalem, desert-brown buildings sprawled in every direction. I checked into my hotel, just blocks from the Old City of Jerusalem, and went for a walk before dinner.

It didn't take long to notice Jerusalem wasn't Tel Aviv. Tel Aviv felt young, busy, self-assured, forward-looking, even happy-go-lucky. Religion wasn't much in evidence. Jerusalem felt conservative, serious, rule-bound and wary. The tension was palpable. Religious symbols were everywhere.

I watched a young couple walking down the street, casually holding hands. The boy carried a rifle slung over his shoulder. The Israeli flag hung from balconies all over the city—something I hadn't seen much in Tel Aviv. I ran into several young girls headed to a costume party. They were dressed in camouflage and pointed their toy rifles at a cat they'd cornered—not a princess in the bunch. A card in my room warned me the hotel observed the Sabbath by taking an elevator out of service, dimming hallway lights, canceling maid service, and shutting down the cappuccino bar. I asked the hotel desk clerk about it and he recited a long list of prohibitions. There were lots of rules.

This is different, I thought.

The next day, I climbed into the car with Beni, my guide. We drove to the Jordan River near Jericho. The energy picked up as we parked and walked down to the river—not much more than a muddy trickle. While Beni talked about John the Baptist and Jesus, I felt the energy of that other life and a sudden jolt. Every cell in my body tingled.

I was here, I thought. *I really was here.*

Now the energy came in waves, one after the other—powerful but manageable.

"Welcome back," M said.

From there we drove north following the river to the tiny, recently-excavated village of Magdala where Beni talked about long-ago everyday life, fishing on the Sea of Galilee, and, of course, Mary Magdalene. We walked to the excavated site of a small synagogue. I again felt the energy of that other life.

I was here too, I thought.

"We were here together," M said.

A jolt of energy nearly brought me to my knees.

"Are you okay?" Beni wanted to know.

"Fine," I said. "Maybe we could sit down somewhere. How about lunch?"

And so it went—from Magdala to Capernaum to Nazareth and back to Jerusalem—something Beni said, something M said, something I saw, something in the air—all familiar. I knew the place and I didn't. Mountains, valleys, Bedouin camps, and date palms. Jordan over there. Syrian refugees over there too. Roman ruins here. Palestinian village next door. Israeli settlement over there. All so close. Energetic nudges and stronger jolts all day long.

That evening, Beni dropped me off at the hotel. I thanked him for a wonderful day and fell into bed.

The next morning, I met Jeremy in the hotel lobby. He was my guide for the Old City of Jerusalem. He started talking before we got out the door. As we walked the narrow cobblestone streets crowded with tourists and trinket shops, Jeremy talked me through thousands of years of history. I was overwhelmed. Near as I could tell, there wasn't a spot on the ground free of blood stains—layer upon layer of blood stains.

The Old City was divided into Quarters among Muslims, Jews, Christians and Armenians and within each of these groups, several different flavors of Muslims, Jews, Christians and Armenians—all warily guarding their patches of bloody ground and coveting the neighbors'. Hostility festered under the skin of the place.

Through that day and the next I walked with Jeremy along the wall around the city, across rooftops from the Jewish Quarter to the Muslim

Quarter, through cemeteries and olive groves to the top of the Mount of Olives and back again. Busloads of tourists swarmed everywhere under the watchful eye of heavily-armed Israeli soldiers.

Late in the afternoon of my second day in the Old City, Jeremy and I waited in line to enter the Church of the Holy Sepulchre, the reputed site of Jesus' empty tomb. I felt the connection to that life as we entered the church. The crowd was intense. Brotherly love was trampled in the pushing and shoving. I felt lightheaded and motioned to Jeremy I was leaving.

"Good," he said. "Thought you'd want to see that. The church is overrun with tourists every afternoon. I'm glad you wanted out. You're here on your own tomorrow, right?"

"Right."

"Come back in the morning if you like. It'll be far easier to wander around if you come early. The church opens at dawn. You'll have the place to yourself."

That night, about midnight, I woke from a nightmare, sweating and out of breath. The bedsheets were drenched. I had no memory of the dream, but I was terrified. I felt the energy of that other life. It consumed me. I was alone. I was lost. I was afraid. The terror was nearly overwhelming.

"Breathe," M said. "Feel this, but know we're here. All is well."

"Your definition of *well* is different from mine. Nothing about this feels *well*. What's the point..."

"Sleep," she said. "The sun will rise soon and a new day will greet you. All is well."

I slept for a little while but woke up—wide awake—before dawn. I took a shower and pulled the clammy sheets off the bed as early morning sunlight inched across the carpet beneath the window. It was 6 o'clock and breakfast wouldn't be served for another couple of hours, so I grabbed a book and sat down to read.

"A walk?" M asked.

"A little early for a walk, don't you think?"

"Goodness, child. You is quite da projec'," Sarah said.

"The church," M encouraged.

"Oh, right," I said. "Good idea."

I put on my shoes and headed for the door. As I walked down the deserted hallway to the elevator, the energy of that other life picked up and ran constantly, smoothly, easily.

I heard clapping and cheering. The Gathered were full of anticipation. I wondered what that was about.

There was nobody on the street. I owned it. I walked through the Jaffa Gate into the Old City and turned left—high stone wall on my left, cobblestone street under my feet, another stone wall on my right. It all felt familiar and it finally hit me, I was living my dream.

Unbelievable, I thought. *Could this be happening?*

With every step the dream came back to me a little clearer. As I approached the huge wooden doors of the church, the door on the right opened. There was nobody around. I stepped inside and heard men chanting but couldn't see them. I walked to the huge domed rotunda and stood looking up at the skylight. Rays of bluish white light bathed the area in front of me, centered on Jesus' tomb.

Energy poured though me. Singing filled my ears. Bells were ringing. Tears streaked my cheeks. I was awestruck.

"Welcome back," M said.

I had nothing to say and if I had, I couldn't have said it.

The most amazing experience of my life, I thought.

"So far," M said.

As the energy subsided, I felt lighter. I'd seen what I needed to see and I'd felt what I needed to feel. The experience was extraordinary.

Back outside, groups of tourists poured down the great stone steps into the church courtyard headed toward me. I made my way through the throng, marveling at the dream and the incredible beauty of living it.

"Okay," I said. "You've got me now. I can't make this stuff up. Lives as Francis and Jesus, prophetic dreams, bridge abutments, and paintings of vaginas? My doubts just evaporated. I'm on board. Where do we go from here?"

"How about breakfast?" M said.

Weaving

MOST MORNINGS WHEN I'm at home, I sit in a small sunroom on the back of the house. A series of windows face the rising sun and the cottage garden. I love looking out those windows while I drink my coffee.

A nice looking gray and white cat hunts in the garden now. His schedule is flexible. I see him every day for a few days and then not at all and then, just as I begin to wonder what's happened to him, he reappears. A juvenile cardinal perches on the back of a chair on the patio looking in the window at me. She's there almost every morning—watching me watching her. Baby rabbits dart around the garden under the watchful eye of their mother who's nibbling the ground cover at the edge of the stone walk. Squirrels chase each other from tree to tree and vibrant blue skinks slink along the window edges looking for an easy meal.

A couple of years ago, as I sat drinking coffee looking out the sunroom windows, a huge tapestry appeared on the wall next to me and remained there just long enough for me to notice without seeing what it depicted. At least ten feet wide and maybe six feet tall, it was heavy and bright with color. It seemed to glow. Rose-colored tassels hung from the corners.

That's all I remember of it. I didn't feel any nudging energy and nobody spoke to me from the ether. It was suddenly there and suddenly gone.

And then one day as I was pressing M for information about what we'd be doing next, she grabbed the microphone and held onto it…

"You love to read, don't you?"

"Sure," I said.

"When you finish a book you love, how do you feel?"

"A little let down…"

"You wish it would go on and on, don't you? You really don't want it to end, do you?"

"Well…"

"You are the main character in a very long book you're writing with your Father. God's got the pen. You're reading the third sentence in the second paragraph on page 68 of a great book that goes on and on. Do you really want it to end? Do you really want to read ahead? Can you enjoy reading that sentence and savor it before moving to the next?

"Okay…"

"Remember the tapestry?"

"Yes, I've been meaning to ask…"

"This life's but one thread in the tapestry," M went on. She was on a roll. When she gets on a roll, she can be hard to interrupt.

"The thread may be short. It may be long. It may be red, or blue or green. It may be made of silk or wool. It is but one thread among many but it is, like every thread, essential to the beauty of the tapestry. Our lives are like that, each beautiful in its own way and each an essential thread in the magnificent tapestry we're creating with our Creator."

"Okay…"

"And each life is unique. No life exactly like any other. Your lives unique to you. My lives unique to me. Each moment in each life bringing us to wherever we are in this moment. Moments we label good or bad or challenging or joyful or sad or happy or empty or overwhelming are, each of them, moments that point to this moment just as it is—each essential to this moment just as it is."

"Well…"

"We are all on the same journey, but each of us is weaving with our Creator a unique story, a magnificent tapestry. Each moment can be lived fully and appreciated for its essential part in the grand story. Please don't miss the moments. They come and go quickly."

"Right..."

"Humankind moves to a time of appreciation for life—all of life. Each loving and appreciating in every moment the great beauty of his life and the great beauty of his neighbor's life and the great beauty of the Earth and all her creatures."

M paused to let all that sink in.

"Perhaps you could enjoy reading the third sentence in the second paragraph on page 68 and let go of the desire to look ahead."

"You've made your point," I said.

"Good," she said.

"Mind if I go to the bathroom now?"

There was no answer.

Big Medicine

"TIME TO GO again," M said. "Time to balance some energies."

"Balance energies? How would I do that?"

"You balance the energies of a place with each step. You changed the energies of Jerusalem just as you've changed the energies of Abadiania, Nashville, Assisi and other places you've walked. Going to these places is more effective than serving them from the comfort of your chair, although that's possible. The energies go where they're needed, but the Earth and its inhabitants benefit from your sensory experience of a place—your presence."

"So the new energy, it touches people…"

"Yes, those open to it, those seeking a new way."

"And it touches the Earth…"

"All is energy. The new energy touches and balances All There Is." She paused.

I'd heard so much remarkable stuff by this point that what she said made sense to me.

"I almost believe you," I said. "Think it's time for the psychiatric ward?"

"How about Sedona? Nice place for a walk. Plenty of crazy people. More fun than going to the hospital."

I'd heard of Sedona, but hadn't been there. It's famous for hiking, mountain biking, thin places, aging hippies, crystal children, and wheatgrass shots. It boasts more massage therapists per square inch than any other place on the planet.

A good place to find a hemp necklace, I thought.

It was early May and already hot. I'd be there for the better part of a week and had planned several long walks, but found I had to get on the trails at sun-up if I wanted to escape the hot afternoon sun. As crowded as Sedona was, the area's trails in the early morning were nearly deserted.

For four days, I hiked through shaded canyons, along rocky ridges, and over the tops of massive buttes. The views were stunning. As far as I could see, the landscape was red rocks, fine-grained sand and rugged desert plants—juniper, yucca, creosote, agave, and a scattering of colorful wildflowers. The sun blazed away in a cloudless, brilliant blue sky. The sunsets were awesome.

Having said all that, I have no idea what the place looked like without sunglasses.

Walking through all the beauty, I fretted. I was in a funk—frustrated with the pace of things again. I'm not the go-getter I was but I still have some go-getting in me. I lapsed into impatience. Sure, I reminded myself to enjoy the moment and sometimes I did. When I did, the world around me slowed and brightened. I was in an amazing place. I could appreciate it. But I'm no spring chicken. I also noticed the hiking was more difficult and my balance not quite what I remembered. I found myself stopping to catch my breath—a lot.

I felt the energies of the place, but they had become such a normal part of life, I didn't think much about them. I will say the energies felt *off*—stagnant, maybe—but I wasn't devoting much attention to them. I wasn't having any of the surprising spiritual experiences touted in the tourist brochures.

"If I'm here to do something, we'd better get on with it. What am I doing here?"

"Patience," M said.

After several days hiking and fretting, I was beat. Time for a day off, but what would I do? In my funk, I couldn't even bring myself to look for a hemp necklace.

A massage, I thought, and felt a sprinkling of energy. The universe liked the idea.

I could have signed up for a massage at the hotel, but instead opened my laptop, looked up *Sedona massage therapists* and got back a landslide of hits—thousands of entries. I picked somebody with lots of experience and lots of stars by her name. Her name was, and still is, Kris.

I lay on her table as she worked my right calf, tight from all the walking. I asked about the FOR SALE sign in her yard. Was she moving?

"I am," she said. "It's a long story."

"I'm not going anywhere," I said.

Months before, Kris felt the call to move from Sedona to Florida to help her aging parents. For the next several months, she searched for an apartment in Florida but didn't find anything she liked. She put her Sedona house up for sale and while every house on the market around her sold within days, her house didn't budge—not even a nibble. She figured she needed a new car to make the trip and called a dealer, but he couldn't locate the car she wanted. She felt blocked, until just a few days before I arrived in Sedona, when everything suddenly changed. She found a place in Florida, her house sold, and the car dealer called to say he'd located her car.

"I realized I was supposed to go to Florida but not until things were ready for me. Now things are ready. I normally don't talk like this when I'm giving a massage, but I felt I needed to tell you this for some reason."

That night I had a dream.

I was driving along a narrow country road. There was a tree-lined open pasture on my left and a road-cut rock wall on my right. The day was bright and sunny. The pasture was green. The trees shaded the road ahead. There weren't any other cars on the road. My window was open to a pleasant breeze.

Suddenly, my tires bogged down in hot asphalt and road equipment was all around me. An old guy in an orange vest driving an asphalt paver looked down at me and shook his head.

I couldn't back up. There was a big truck behind me. I couldn't drive ahead without messing up the steaming asphalt. And I couldn't stay where I was. So I drove ahead slowly scoring deep ruts in the fresh asphalt while all the guys in orange vests shook their heads.

After a hundred yards or so, I found myself on a section of road graveled but not yet paved.

Good, I thought. *Glad to be out of that mess.*

And that's when the road ended abruptly at the edge of an overgrown gully marked with a strand of rusted barbed-wire. I was stuck again.

Good lord, I thought. *Now what?*

Something caught my attention and I turned to see the road didn't actually end. It curved sharply to the right and rose straight up into the sky—graveled and ready to be paved as far up as I could see.

Another guy in an orange vest walked over to my car.

"Hey mister," he said. "This road's closed. It's being paved."

"I can see that. What do I do? I'm stuck here."

"Well, you'll have to wait till the road gets paved and you're going to need a different car to drive up that stretch over there," he shook his head. "There's no way this car's going up that."

I woke up.

"Impatient?" M asked.

"A little."

"A lot," M said. "Your energy for doing will serve you when it's time. The road is being paved and…"

"I know," I interrupted. "I'm getting a new vehicle. A bigger boat."

"Right. Maybe you'd like to go back to sleep now. Someone's waiting for you."

Another dream…

I walked in a field of waist-high grass toward a dry creek. I couldn't see much. The night was dark. As I came to the rocky streambed, I could barely make out the low ridge of the bank on the far side. There was a big tree on the ridge and someone was behind the tree. A man, I thought. With a hat of some sort. Native American. A medicine man.

Why I thought those things, I don't know. I couldn't see him very well. He was mostly hidden behind the tree's massive trunk.

I crossed the streambed and climbed up the low bank. I stood in the dark looking at the tree, trying to see.

A shadowy figure came out from behind the tree and stood briefly before sprinting toward me and WHAM, he came into me through my chest—at least that's the way it felt. I staggered backward and stood for a moment before I woke up.

And went immediately back to sleep.

More dreaming…

I was standing in Sandy's treatment room in Nashville in the dark. I felt I should lie down on her treatment table. I knew something needed to be adjusted. I put my hands on the table edge and WHAM, my whole body jerked. I tingled with intense energy and…

I woke up, still tingling.

"The shaman's energy," M said.

"Who…"

"In time," she said, "you will know."

"Why all the mystery?"

There was no answer. I lay there for a bit as the tingling faded.

Getting a new vehicle and waiting for the road to be paved, I thought. *I keep hearing that. And now a shaman's energy.*

"God got da pen," Sarah said. "You in awful good hands."

→═◎ ◎═←

After I wrote what you've just read, I called Kris to see how Florida was treating her. "Funny you should call. It's time for me to go back to Sedona," she said. "I understand why I came to Florida. The last year has been important for me—not what I expected, but what I needed. I've done what I came to do here and now it's time to go back. When are you coming to Sedona?"

"I don't have any plans right now, but that doesn't mean much."

"Hah, so true," she said, laughing.

Waiting

IN MY OLD life chasing the American Dream, I was paid to make things happen and get things done. Doing was my way of living. A free moment was an opportunity to move something forward, even if only a little bit. Push, push, push....

After my trip to Sedona, I entered another time of waiting. Serov explained there was a lot being prepared. Others would be doing. I would be watching mostly and doing some traveling. We weren't losing time, he said.

Often the fastest way forward is allowing things to unfold without pushing. While the road was being paved, I'd be assimilating the energies of other lives—getting my new vehicle.

Thereafter, I had a series of dreams about *waiting*.

One of them…

I'm waiting at the white door of a small building. I'm not sure why I'm there but I'm early and the door's locked.

I wake up, remember the dream and go back to sleep.

I'm back at the door waiting for it to open. It's still not time.

I wake up, remember the dream and go back to sleep.

I'm back at the door. It's late afternoon and time for the door to open. I ring the doorbell and the door opens for me. I walk into a restaurant. There's nobody there.

Tables are set for a dinner, a celebration of some sort—white tables, white chairs, white tablecloths, white walls, white candles.

Unfortunately I'm way too early. The tables are set, but it's not time for dinner.

I wake up.

And while I was *waiting*, there were dreams about *preparation*.

One of them…

My body is fitted inside a large wooden frame—like a picture frame—and I'm stretched comfortably corner to corner.

I'm suddenly out of my body, viewing myself from above. I see myself inside the frame. There are several people moving busily around the frame. I'm invited down to see the frame from the side. I'm composed of layers—one on top of the other. The layers already in place have place names—Assisi, Jerusalem, Sedona. There are spaces inside the frame for 5 more places. The people there are readying me to fill these empty spaces. The next space will be filled soon.

I wake up.

"Patience." M said.

→══ ══←

Waiting is a big part of my journey. I was reminded of this a couple of months ago when a pair of robins built a nest in the Jackson vine above the loveseat on my front porch. It's where I sit in the evening after a long day of waiting and wait some more.

The robins didn't ask. There was no discussion about rent or rules. They took the space, built their nest and moved in while my back was turned. I didn't know what'd happened till I sat down on my porch sofa one night and noticed momma staring down at me from the nest. She'd already pooped—more than once—on the old wooden chest where I prop my feet.

This'll never do, I thought. *This nest has to go…*

But I caught myself and reminded myself that I am now a spiritual person and this is one of God's creatures and God is creating new life with these creatures and I can participate in this creation by allowing them to stay.

Oh bother, I thought.

As the robins sat on their nest, waiting for two little blue eggs to hatch, they grew more protective of the space around them. They were expansionists. If I sat on the porch, momma robin squawked while dad swooped around my head. I was not permitted to sit on the porch. So I ceded space and moved to the cottage porch.

When the chicks hatched, I wasn't even allowed to come and go through the front door. So I ceded more space. I came and went through the back door.

This went on for weeks till one day when I pulled into my driveway and a robin chick fluttered awkwardly onto the hood of my car. He looked at me through the windshield, confused and a little lost, before flying to the plum tree next door. The nest was empty. The robin family had moved on.

They showed me how to wait. They created *and* held space till something new came along—until it was time to move on. I tried to be grateful to them while I scrubbed bird shit off the wooden chest.

It's only after a period of waiting that Serov appears and says "It's time." Waiting ends and I move forward, until the next time of waiting.

The Dreamtime

"Like your paintings, your dreams show the way," M said. "They're an easy way to communicate with you. You're entering another time of dreaming. You'll have help—a new healer. She's coming soon."

"She's French," Sandy said, as I lay on her table. "No, maybe European. But there's something French about her. She's coming now."

A few days later, I lay on Bonnie's table. "I've been asked to give you the name of one of my students. Her name is Jule. She teaches dreamwork."

And a couple of weeks later, "Jule is French or Dutch for Jewel. I was born in this country but my roots are Dutch."

Damn, I thought. *That was fast.*

My dreamlife took off again. Jule and I met every few weeks. She taught me a lot. As she became more familiar with my dreams and the rest of my story, including some of my paintings, she noticed something.

"Are you familiar with Hildegard? Hildegard of Bingen?" Jule asked.

Energy buzzed through me when I heard the name.

"I don't know her name," I said, "but I don't get an energy rush like that unless there's some connection."

"Hildegard was a Christian mystic, born in Germany and raised in the Catholic Church," Jule said. "She enjoyed a rich dreamlife, visions, painting, and composing music. She studied the healing properties of plants, talked to God, and wrote about it. She was an amazing woman. You might enjoy reading about her."

A few nights later, I had this dream:

From high above, I was watching a sleek, high speed train glide over open pastureland, around a big bend, into a narrow valley. A river ran through the valley and the train tracks followed the river. The river was wide and the valley's hillsides were dotted with vineyards. It was a beautiful place and familiar somehow.

In the dream I thought, *Germany. This looks like Germany.*

The dream shifted and I was the train, moving through the valley alongside the river. I was carrying just one passenger. She sat alone in one of my cars. She was quietly, naturally beautiful—casually dressed in light-brown hiking pants, a dark green shirt and river-walk sandals. She sat looking out the window as we moved fast but silently through the countryside. Her name was Holi.

The dream shifted and I was sitting beside her. The two of us were the only passengers on the train. Holi felt comfortable, like we'd been together for a very long time. She was calm and easy. We weren't talking. We were just riding together—being together.

The dream shifted. Holi and I were at a banquet. The table was being set for us. There were others there—milling about, waiting. They were wearing white robes and seemed to glow from within. Their light was so bright I couldn't make out their faces, but they were friends and were having a good time.

Holi and I walked around while we waited for the banquet to start. It was a grand hotel filled with warm white light streaming from huge chandeliers. We wandered into a room where two guards were strapping four scruffy naked men to a large wooden pallet. The naked guys were tough-looking, cursing and spitting at their jailers but not otherwise resisting. The guards finished their work and raised the pallet onto its side so the naked guys were facing us, still sneering and cursing. The guards lifted the pallet and hauled the naked guys away.

146

"I've seen enough of that energy to last me a lifetime," Holi said. "Can we go back to the party?"

"Sure. Maybe the table's set."

It was.

As we entered the banquet room, our light-filled friends laughed and applauded. "We've been waiting for you. You must select the wine."

The table offered up a sumptuous feast—cheeses, dark breads, raw vegetables and sauces, a variety of smoked fishes, sausages and other meats. The wine steward handed me the wine list. It was written in German. I handed it to Holi and said, "It's time for you to choose the wine. I'm sure whatever you choose will be delicious."

The wine steward brought Holi's selections to the table. Wine glasses were there—delicate crystal for the white wine and sturdier crystal for the red.

"I chose, you pour," Holi said. She was stunningly beautiful.

I poured the white wine. We raised our glasses and drank. Nothing was said. The wine was deliciously crisp and fruity, but not sweet. Heads nodded approval all around the table, but still nothing was said. It felt like a ceremony of some sort—like a wedding, maybe.

I poured the red wine. There were enough fresh glasses for all but one of us. So after I poured the remaining glasses, I started to pour red wine into my white wine glass where there was still a sip of wine in the bottom. There was an uproar of objection from our robed friends, but I said, "If the red is as good as the white, the two together can only be better."

Holi smiled.

We all raised our glasses and drank. The wine was bold and earthy. It was delicious.

The room erupted in laughter and clapping.

"It's time," I said to Holi.

She nodded. "Yes, it's time."

I woke up, buzzing with energy.

"And?" M said.

"I'm going to Germany to touch my life as Hildegard."

"Yes," M said. "Isn't this fun?"

→▶─ ◉▆◀─

I landed in Frankfurt and boarded a fast train to Bingen, a tiny village on the Rhine River where the great wide river bends north and flows through the steep-sided Rhine River Valley, famous for its vineyards and wineries. I planned to walk through the hills on either side of the river from Bingen to Koblenz, but before leaving Bingen I wanted to visit sites where Hildegard lived and walked.

The Benedictine Abbey of St. Hildegard sits high on a hill overlooking the town of Rudesheim, just a short ferry ride across the river from Bingen. I walked from the ferry dock into Rudesheim and found my way to a well-marked path meandering through vineyards uphill to a catholic parish church that sits on the foundation of the convent Hildegard founded in 1165. From there, I planned to hike up to the abbey at the top of the hill, then along the hilltop through vineyards tended by the nuns, and back downhill into Rudesheim.

As I approached the small parish church, energy ran powerfully but easily through me. It was a cloudy morning, the sun breaking through from time to time. I stood on the edge of a one lane road leading to the church and looked across the vineyards back toward Rudesheim and the broad river beyond.

I was here, I thought. The energy running through me flashed powerfully and settled back down. The closer I walked to the church, the stronger the energy ran.

Two women were in the cemetery outside the church tending a grave.

"Remember," Grace said. "This is where it happens."

"You're back," I said. "Haven't heard from you in a while."

The women in the churchyard smiled and waved as I approached, pointing around the corner to the front of the church. A busload of tourists were leaving. When I walked in, the sanctuary was empty. The energy stopped running as I took off my backpack and sat down in a pew.

"This is not where it happens," Grace said.

I sat for a few minutes, but felt no connection to the church. I put a few coins in the collection box in the foyer and walked back the way I came. As soon as I started down the church steps to the cemetery, the energy picked up again and ran smoothly.

"This is where it happens," Grace said.

⤜◉ ◉⤛

There's a lot more I could say about that day. The abbey at the top of the hill is well worth a visit and the walk through the vineyards back down to Rudesheim is delightful. I heartily recommend both, but I need to move along.

For the next several days, I walked the hills along the Rhine River from village to village on my way to Koblenz, about 70 miles north, following generally well-marked paths.

By the fourth day, I was predictably tired. On all my trips, I'd been engaged and busy for a few days before tiredness set in and I started thinking about a day off. Germany was no exception.

"Follow yo' heart," Sarah said. "What yo' heart want?"

I was in my hotel room in the village of St. Goar. I'd just eaten breakfast and was looking over my maps for the day's walk to Kamp-Bornhofen. My enthusiasm was waning.

"I don't know," I said.

Maybe you'd like to sit and listen," M suggested. "Listen to your heart. It knows." It was another instruction masquerading as a suggestion.

So I sat in a chair facing the window, looking out onto the well-kept village. I was tired and a little down. Another day of walking alone in the hills wasn't appealing to me.

"You never alone, child," Sarah said.

Suddenly I saw Pope Francis, wearing a white cassock and skull cap, walking toward me from the window. He stopped in front of me and bowed slightly, smiling. He motioned for me to stay seated, so I bowed from my chair and smiled back.

Wow, I thought.

He moved next to me, standing on my right, facing the window.

The Dalai Lama—bald, smiling brightly, wearing a simple saffron robe—walked toward me from the window. He too stopped in front of me, bowed slightly and motioned for me to stay in my chair. I bowed and smiled back. He came and stood beside me on my left facing the window.

And so it went. Francis came and stood next to the Pope. Jesus came and stood next to the Dalai Lama. The Hopi shaman came and stopped a few feet in front of me. He crouched down on the floor, doing something with his hands, smiling at me but not showing what he was doing. And then a woman wearing a plain white nun's habit walked up in front of me and smiled. She was young and radiantly beautiful.

"Hildegard," I said, bowing slightly.

She bowed and came to stand next to me where Pope Francis made a space for her.

A whole host of light-filled beings now came toward us from the window—thousands of them led by M, Sarah, Grace and Serov—singing a hymn in a language I didn't know. They surrounded us on all sides as the Hopi shaman rose to show me a small fire he'd built in his cupped hand.

Lord, I thought, *the smoke alarm...*

He blew out the fire and held smoking embers under my nose until I inhaled the smoke twice. My body jerked with each inhalation. My scalp tingled. Weariness lifted off me. I felt light and exquisitely happy—and relieved the fire alarm hadn't gone off.

There was laughter and applause all around.

"We walk together," M said. "We're always with you. We are legion. We are the Gathering."

"Now what yo' heart wantin'?" Sarah asked.

"I think I'll walk to the coffee shop, have a cup of coffee, and take a tour boat to my next stop. We'll see what happens from there."

"Good, child. Real good."

An hour later, I sat at a small table on the deck of a Rhine River tour boat drinking coffee. The day was gorgeous—sunny and cool with a light breeze coming off the water. I rode for nearly an hour taking it all in. (One of these days, I'll take another of those boat rides. I thoroughly enjoyed it.)

At Kamp-Bornhofen I walked through town to the Hotel Becker. Several people I met along the way recommended it's restaurant. I was a little early for lunch, but a beautiful young waitress showed me to a table overlooking the street and brought me a glass of the local wine. She spoke English and had an engaging smile. When the kitchen opened, she handed me a menu, but recommended the cheeseburger.

"Our cheeseburger is excellent," she said. "Americans love it."

"Good. I'll have the cheeseburger. No hurry. I'm content to sit and look out the window. It's beautiful here. And I'll have another glass of wine."

My heart was doing what it truly loves to do.

Steve Johnson

For the moment, I was the only diner. I had a great view down the cobblestone street to the river. I watched the river traffic and the trains and the walkers and the bikers. People came and went from the shops along the street. I ate my cheeseburger. It was excellent. And I enjoyed the wine. Toward the end of the meal, a couple of elderly women came walking up the street. One was on crutches. She moved slowly in obvious pain. Her companion patiently walked beside her, helping her navigate the cobblestones.

I wish she could walk more comfortably, I thought.

"She can," Grace said.

"What?"

"Time to wear the robe if you're willing to put it on."

About that time, the two ladies came into the restaurant and sat down at a nearby table. I turned and nodded to them. They smiled and nodded back.

"Time to wear the robe? What do you mean?" I asked.

"You know," Grace said. "Trust your knowing."

It was then I noticed an older couple walking up the street toward me. The man was on crutches. His wife (or so I assumed) walked beside him, helping as he too navigated the cobblestones.

"Can he walk more comfortably?"

"He can," Grace said. "Time to wear the robe."

I felt energy pick up and run through me steadily as the couple entered the restaurant and sat at a table near the two ladies.

"You know how to do this," Grace said. "Trust your knowing, open your heart to them, and allow the energy to flow. It will."

Am I willing to do this? I wondered.

Doubt nagged at me. What would I do? What would I say?

Good lord, I thought. *Just get up and do it.*

Energy poured through me. I got up from my table after paying the bill. I asked the young waitress if she'd translate and I turned first to the lady on crutches. The words came.

"You'll walk easier," I said, energy still pouring through me.

Both ladies looked at me, their mouths open. It seemed ages before the lady on crutches said her knee was broken and she was in a lot of pain.

"I can see that," I said, "You'll walk easier."

The energy picked up even more and came in pulsing waves.

"Now the gentleman," Grace said.

So I turned to the older man on crutches. He and his wife had been listening to my conversation with the ladies.

I smiled and said, "You'll walk easier too."

The man looked incredulous, but his wife beamed. Her eyes glistened with tears.

I looked at the man again and nodded, "You'll walk easier."

This time he smiled and the energy pulsed through me as it had with the ladies.

"Bless you," his wife said. She took my hand and held it. "Bless you."

The energy continued pulsing for a few seconds before subsiding.

The waitress stood looking at me wide-eyed, holding my backpack. I took it, thanked her for the wonderful meal, waved to the couples and walked toward the door before turning around and asking," Does anyone know the Hotel Burg Liebenstein?"

The waitress walked me to the front door and pointed straight up, "The castle. It's up there."

It was. Way up there.

Oh bother, I thought.

"Wearin' da robe, child. You rememberin'," Sarah said.

"Welcome back," Grace said.

Hope

A COUPLE OF months before my trip to Germany, I had an odd dream:

I was holding a padlock—the kind with a dial that goes on a gym locker—trying to remember the combination. It was a lock I had in high school. Somehow it found its way into the back of a drawer in my desk. Surprisingly the combination was still there in the deep dusty recesses of my brain: 11-27-15. I tried the combination and it worked. The lock opened. I knew I needed to remember the combination but didn't know why. I repeated 11-27-15 over and over to myself.

I woke up, still repeating the numbers 11-27-15.

And then, two months later, when I arrived in Koblenz at the end of my Germany trip, I had this dream:

I was walking along a path through a large pasture, carrying a tall gym locker that was locked with a padlock. I didn't have the combination. I wished I could open it. It was full of something heavy that seemed to move around, constantly shifting its weight. I needed to rest so I set the locker down. I sat in front of it looking at the padlock and suddenly remembered the dream I'd had months before—the combination was 11-27-15.

I tried it and the locker door swung open. The locker was full of *hope*. It flowed—gold in color and the consistency of honey—from the locker and all over the pasture in every direction to the horizon.

I woke up.

"It's what you bring," M said. "You bring hope. You've opened the door and it flows now, in every direction."

She paused, then asked, "How was your trip?"

"Beautiful," I said.

"Worth waiting for?"

"Yes, worth the wait. I'd like to come back someday."

"Good," she said.

Seeing Clearly

I ENTERED *ANOTHER* time of waiting—another opportunity to work with patience. You can imagine how grateful I was.

During the next few months, I underwent cataract surgery in both eyes, lost Yoda, and weathered a withering bout of flu. Oh joy.

The cataract surgery went well but consumed the better part of two months. I'm glad I did it. The world is a brighter, clearer place now, but two months of downtime left me antsy.

As my eyesight recovered, Yoda declined. I knew it was time for him to go, but the days following his departure were challenging. I woke to let him out. He wasn't there. I got up from my chair to let him in. He wasn't there. I thought about filling his water bowl. I didn't need to.

So it went for weeks. I missed him terribly.

And then I got the flu, gave it to everybody I knew, and played layabout for another month. I felt awful.

When I wasn't recovering or grieving or whining about the injustice of it all, I was waiting. None of it felt very spiritual. The whole thing put me in a foul mood or should I say, *another* foul mood. Even I was beginning to notice a pattern.

I tried—briefly—to remember all the beautifully wise words about waiting and enjoying the moment and impermanence and patience, but, as I've said before, remembering and living are two different things. I still had a ways to go on the *living* part.

Employing their great wisdom and broader perspective, M and the others let me sulk. I guess they were tired of talking about it.

And then one night, I had this dream:

I was at an outdoor barbecue with family and friends before walking into an unexplored land. I could see it from the top of the hill where we were eating grilled chicken and corn on the cob. My dad was cautioning me not to go, saying we need you here and nobody's ever gone there before. The trip would be dangerous.

"I'll be fine, I said. "And someday I'll be back. But now I have to go. God is telling me it's time to go."

So I took another bite of chicken and walked downhill into the new world. It was lush green hills and beautiful dense forests with paths through them. I didn't see other people, but animals were everywhere. They walked with me. I talked to them and they followed me, some leaving, others arriving and walking with me for a while. I lay down to rest in the grass.

I woke up.

"Time to go again," Grace said. "Things are speeding up for you now. You have other lives to touch. Pay attention. Your heart knows the way."

Within weeks, I knew I'd be visiting with Leonardo da Vinci and St. Patrick.

Lunch

PAOLA, MY GUIDE for the day, met me at the hotel first thing Sunday morning. The Italian sky was Mediterranean blue. The morning was sunny and warm.

Florence teemed with tourists. Stepping out the front door of the hotel was like stepping into line. I don't much care for standing in line. I'd just arrived. I was jet-lagged and suffering from a puzzling case of gut-clenching anxiety. My body was bracing for something, but what? The crowds weren't making things easier.

As we walked, I explained to Paola I'd been to Florence a couple of times and had seen most of the tourist sites, but wanted to go back to the Uffizi Gallery to see the few works of Leonardo da Vinci on display there—in particular, *The Annunciation*, depicting the angel Gabriel announcing to Mary that she was going to give birth to Jesus.

"Why that painting?" Paola asked.

"I don't know," I said. "I'm drawn to it. I've seen pictures but I've not seen the painting itself."

"Okay," she said. "But there's so much more to see…"

I stopped her.

"Paola, I don't want to offend you but I've already seen much of Florence. Can you take me to see that painting? We can figure out where to go from there."

"Okay, but take a look at the façade of this building while we're here…"

"Paola…"

"Yes, of course, but you've booked me for the day and there's so much…"

"Paola…"

"The Uffizi," she said. "Leonardo da Vinci."

"Good," I said.

We made a beeline for the Uffizi where we stood in the fast line—a very long line. Paola pointed to the slow line. It was way longer than the fast line, but knowing that was small comfort.

Inside, Paola commenced stopping at every painting along the way. She was in the middle of exercising her vast knowledge for my benefit when I held up my hand and said," Paola…"

"But Steve, I hate for you to come all this way and not see…"

"I know you do, but I'd like to see the Leonardo painting and go to lunch and I'd like you to join me for lunch."

"Do you have…"

"Yes, I have. Trattoria Cammillo…"

"Cammillo? I've never been. It's quite a good restaurant."

"A friend recommended it."

"Okay," Paola said, eyes brightening. Suddenly, we were off and running. Paola was a tour guide on a mission: show the impatient American his painting and go to lunch. It was something a good Italian could get into. We didn't stop again until I sat on a bench looking at Leonardo's painting, *The Annunciation*.

It's a good thing I was sitting. As Paola weighed in on the painting and its history, a tsunami of energy hit me in the chest—*WHAM!*

If I'd been standing, I'd have fallen backwards into Paola's lap. Thank goodness she knew a lot about the painting. Her vast knowledge gave me a few minutes to recover before moving on.

We walked into the next room where we sat again and watched a film about the restoration of another of Leonardo's paintings, *Adoration of the Magi*. It too was spectacular and the film was fascinating. I felt the energy of the painting, but nothing like what I'd experienced with *The Annunciation* just moments before.

As the film wrapped up, I was hungry—really hungry. I leaned toward Paola and whispered, "How about lunch?"

I didn't have to repeat myself.

Back outside, I glimpsed Michelangelo's *David* as Paola navigated the madding crowd and pointed toward the Arno, where just the other side of the Ponte Santa Trinita, we walked into family-run Trattoria Cammillo and ate a wonderful, leisurely lunch—easily one of the best meals I've ever eaten. Gregarious Paola made it her business to meet the family while we waited for our food and introduced me to all of them. Family photos came off the wall and stories were told—all in animated Italian. I nodded and smiled a lot. The experience was delightful.

After lunch, walking back across the bridge, I felt the Leonardo energy rising in me. It was frenetic and unsettling. It was exhausting.

"Paola, I think I'd better go back to the hotel. I'm feeling tired all of a sudden. I need to take a nap."

"Of course, if you're tired we can head that way but before…"

"Paola…"

"Okay, okay," she said, waving her arms. "To the hotel."

I went to my room and lay down. Twelve hours later, I woke up at 3 o'clock in the morning, agitated—severely agitated. I'd never felt anything like it. I couldn't sleep, eat, read or sit still. I paced.

I was bored and, I think, a little depressed. I didn't want to be there anymore. I'd done what I came to do. I'd connected to Leonardo's energy. I didn't care to see more of Florence. I'd seen it. I wanted out and there was no getting out, certainly not at that time of the morning. I'm glad nobody was there with me. I was not a person anybody'd want to be around.

I struggled with agitation and boredom until dawn and all through the next day. I could hardly wait to get on the train to Lucca where I planned to spend a few days before going on to Rome. I'd never been to Lucca. It was new—at least it was to me—and smaller, less crowded. I desperately wanted to see something new, experience something new.

It was my second night in Lucca before it dawned on me I was still fighting with Leonardo's energy. I wasn't myself. His energy had taken me over.

As I walked the top of the wall surrounding the beautiful little town of Lucca—around and around—I thought about Leonardo. No wonder he was so peripatetic. With his frenetic energy, settling down was not an option. No wonder he couldn't finish things. Once he saw where a project was going, finishing was drudgery. I felt what he felt intensely and I realized his fear of standing still was greater than his fear of stepping into the unknown or what others thought of him. His creative drive— his craving for the new—was fueled in part by his fear of standing still. He knew he couldn't bear it. He'd spiral into depression or worse.

That's what I was feeling. That was the root of my agitation and boredom.

And that led to understanding I have a bit of Leonardo's energy in me too—not to the degree he embodied it—but enough to propel me forward. I faced my own fear of standing still and understood it helps fuel my willingness to step into this journey—to embrace the possibilities of this life—no matter how challenging the swirl. It serves a purpose. It's part of who I am.

When I got home, folks asked about my trip to Italy.

"It was a bitch," I said, and that was true except for lunch at Cammillo. Lunch was exceptional.

Luck O' the Irish

SHORTLY AFTER ITALY, I was headed to Ireland for a 10-day tour of sacred sites with my guide, Liam. I'd been to Ireland once before and loved it. I wanted to see more—particularly places associated with St. Patrick—and I was delighted to be doing something after another period of waiting.

A week or so before the trip, I lay on Sandy's table. An overzealous yoga move messed with my back and the pain was breathtaking. I needed help. M had asked me to take some Hildegard music with me so Sandy could play it while she worked on me. I chose a collection of Hildegard pieces interpreted by Richard Souther. As a piece he calls *The Anointing* played, Sandy abruptly stopped work on my back, stepped back from the table for a moment, retrieved a small bottle of frankincense oil, and dabbed a bit of it on my forehead, heart, and feet. As the music faded, I asked what she'd done.

"An anointing, Steve. I was asked to anoint you. So sacred. I was filled with a beautiful energy and guided each step."

Now we both felt the beautiful energy Sandy had enjoyed. It seemed to fill the room around us.

"Another anointing? Think of that, Sandy. It's going to take a bunch of blessings to erase my unholy past."

"Or open a door," M suggested.

"St. Patrick is here," Sandy said.

"I wondered when we'd meet him."

"He's here," Sandy said. "It's up to you what you want to do."

"I'm ready."

Within seconds, St. Patrick's energy came into me. I felt a powerful soft energy radiate from my heart and fill the room around us. St. Patrick was on board and I hadn't gotten on a plane yet. It was his energy Sandy and I had experienced during the anointing. It was now part of me.

As I was leaving Sandy's, she placed a small piece of wood in my hand.

"This is Druid wood. A friend gave it to me long ago. It's a treasure to me. I'm asked to give it to you to carry with you on your trip."

I saw the concern in her face.

"I'll be careful with it," I said, putting her treasure in my pocket.

"Thank you," Sandy said. "I'm told you'll take my piece of wood along with a few other things."

"Other things?"

"You'll know," she said.

A couple of days later, I was in the cottage painting, allowing my hands to move light blues and greens over the canvas without having any idea what would appear there. An hour later I stepped back to see a path winding around a rocky outcrop down to the sea.

"Where you're going," M said. "To make a connection to your life in Jerusalem. You have something you brought back from Israel."

"I didn't buy anything…" I started, but remembered a small coin I'd found in the bottom of my suitcase after the trip.

"Yes," M said. "If you will, please take the coin with you along with Sandy's Druid wood, a small crystal from Brazil, and your clam shell."

For nearly 30 years I've carried a clam shell in my pocket—one I found on top of a mountain in Montana. It reminds me every day how old the Earth is and how little time I have here.

"Right," I said. "What will I do with this?"

"You'll know," M said.

--▪▸◉◼◉◂▪--

Arrival day in Dublin was recovery day. I walked the city to move my stiff joints after the long flight. My body has an unfortunate memory of flying around on airplanes during my business career and doesn't care to repeat any of it. The jet lag wasn't helping either. So I walked without a destination in mind, just following my nose.

Dublin is a friendly, wonderfully clean city. It was Sunday and the sun was shining. It seemed all the inhabitants were out enjoying the good weather. The restaurants were full, street musicians sang for their supper, old folks lined park benches and young couples smooched on blankets in the grass. The city felt comfortable and in places, familiar.

In the early afternoon I came to an inviting park and wandered through it. As I did, energy tingled in the top of my head. I was connecting to something, but what? I wondered about this until I came to a plaque that said *St. Patrick's Park,* where it's believed St. Patrick baptized the first Irish Christians.

Yep, I thought. *That's true.*

"Welcome back," M said.

I walked on and soon discovered another beautiful park, St. Stephens Green. Clouds swirled overhead playing with the sunlight so the vibrant greens of Ireland could show themselves. Again the energy picked up and tingled in the top of my head. I was connecting to something new.

A young woman on a park bench just ahead sat with a girl in a wheelchair who clung to a soft pillow and rocked herself to music only she could hear. I nodded to them as I passed by and thought about the challenges they faced together.

"Time to wear the robe," M said.

"Really? What…"

"You know. Trust your knowing."

I turned around and went back to them. Energy coursed through me as it had in Kamp-Bornhofen. As I approached, the girl in the wheelchair looked up at me and brightened. Her caretaker was less sure. The energy poured through me as I said "This girl is an angel."

Her caretaker's skepticism turned into a smile. "Yes," she said. "She is."

"Here," I said, handing the caretaker a few Euros. "Maybe you'd both enjoy some ice cream."

"I can't..." the caretaker started.

"Yes, you can," I said.

"Thank you," she said. "This angel loves ice cream."

The young girl smiled.

"Good. Seeing the two of you has brightened my day. Thank you. Enjoy your ice cream."

The energy subsided and I walked on.

"Wearing the robe," M said. "Your presence is all that's needed. No doing. Only allowing. Remember who you are."

Liam picked me up the next morning and we were off. I quickly discovered he had an encyclopedic knowledge of Irish history and the country's sacred sites. I was riding with the right guy. We visited Patrick's first church, a spring where he bathed, and the area where he was held captive by a Celtic chieftain—all in the north of Ireland—and in each place I felt the connection to that other life as I had in Dublin. My body struggled a bit with each connection, but recovered quickly—receiving the energy in small bites. His energy felt strong, even sturdy, but soft— just as it had at Sandy's.

Over the next several days we visited the passage tombs of Carrowkeel, Poulnabrone dolmen, and several stone circles, including the small Uragh stone circle perched on a lush grassy hill between two crystal clear lakes. If there's a more peaceful place on the planet,

I haven't experienced it. Liam and I stayed a good while, enjoying the silence of the circle and the wild beauty of its setting.

While Liam was off exploring a nearby hill, Grace asked me to step into the circle and walk its inside edge. As I walked, she talked.

"In your life as Jesus, you walked well outside the circle. You made a show of defying cultural and institutional norms and lost your life."

She let that sink in.

"In several lives thereafter—your lives as Hildegard and Patrick for example—you stepped back into the circle and walked the outside of the inside of the circle as you are doing now. You were part of the Catholic Church and managed to live just inside acceptable institutional norms—often testing the limits of institutional and cultural patience but keeping your head."

She paused.

"If you will, step outside the circle now and walk around its outer edge, touching each stone as you pass."

I did as I was asked.

"In this life you've chosen again to walk outside the circle but you walk a bit closer to it—the inside of the outside. You're not affiliated with any institution or group. You have no tribe. You walk outside cultural and institutional norms but not defiantly. In this life you quietly deliver a gift that challenges long-held beliefs and the people and institutions that rely on them for their power. As you walk and people come to understand who you are, the swirl around you will increase. It will be intense at times, but you will walk through it quietly, delivering your gift through your presence. You are well prepared."

I stopped walking and stood gazing at the waterfall that feeds the lakes below Uragh circle. Grace read my thoughts and laughed.

"Aware, not afraid. This time around the circle, you will keep your head."

"Good to know," I said.

→═◎ ◎═←

Toward the end of the trip, Liam and I planned to take a boat trip to Skellig Michael, a rocky crag 7 miles off Ireland's Iveragh peninsula where some determined monks built a small monastery in the 6th century. It was occupied until the monks got their fill of Viking raids and moved to a replacement monastery in the village of Ballinskelligs on the mainland, abandoning their wind-blown, rocky retreat.

As we checked out of the hotel on the morning of our boat trip, Liam got a call from the boat captain saying the seas were rough and we wouldn't be sailing. Liam's disappointment was obvious. He'd been before and, knowing my love of wild places, wanted me to experience one of the wildest places in Ireland.

"No worries," I said. "Maybe we're to see something else."

"How about driving on to Portmagee where we were planning to meet the boat? You might enjoy a walk around the village. We can explore from there."

"Sounds good. Do you suppose we could find a walking path along the coast? I'd love a long walk."

"Let's see," Liam said. " I'll get the car."

While Liam was away, M spoke up.

"Trust your knowing," she said.

"There's another place I'm to visit."

"Yes. Your painting. Ask for help along the way. Let go of your tendency to go it alone. Others are there to help you if you ask."

Liam and I drove to Portmagee, found a coffee shop, and settled into a nice view of the small harbor and a cappuccino. I'd shown Liam a picture of my painting. I felt we'd find the place shown in the painting and we'd know it when we got there. While we sat, we quizzed our friendly waitress on places to see and things to do in the area.

"Oooh," she said. "Have you been to Ballinskelligs?"

"No," Liam said.

"Oh, you must see Ballinskelligs—the abbey ruins. And there's a lovely walk along the beach. It's my favorite place."

As she talked, I felt a strong energetic nudge.

"What do you think?" I asked Liam.

"Sure. We can drive the coast road. On the way, maybe you'll get a glimpse of Skellig Michael. Looks like that's as close as we're going to get today."

Our waitress beamed. "You'll love it," she said.

The drive along the coast to Balinskelligs was breathtaking. The weather was frothy and the sea surged in great swells crashing along the rock cliffs below us.

Lord, I thought. *I'd be seasick for a month if we'd gone out on the boat.*

"You're welcome," M said.

A mile or so before we descended into Ballinskelligs, we turned a corner around a small rise and the sea came into view.

"The painting," I said. "It's the painting."

"So it is," Liam said.

"We're where we need to be."

We parked at the abbey ruins and got out to wander around. We walked between the grave markers that fill the 10th century ruin and stood at a stone wall looking out to sea.

"The coin," M said.

"Yes. The shekel."

I thought about Jerusalem and that lifetime. Now Ireland and another lifetime. So mysterious and yet it all seemed normal to me. I knew what to do.

I tossed the coin into the sea.

"Nice," M said. "Simply done. Liam will move the car now. Perhaps you'd like to stay here by yourself for a bit."

"I'm going to move the car," Liam said. "Stay and enjoy this. I'll be back shortly."

Goodness, I thought. *I can't make this stuff up.*

As Liam walked away, M said, "You have Sandy's Druid wood, the crystal and your clam shell."

"In my pocket."

"You know what to do," M said.

I did. I lay the three pieces on the wall—the piece of Druid wood on the left, the clam shell on the right and the crystal between them. The three pieces sat nested together. I stood back a step and looked out across the sea. Energy tingled in the top of my head and poured through me like a raging river into the ground. It was a powerful ceremony of some sort. I knew how to do it. I performed it. But I didn't understand it.

"What was that about?" I asked.

"Allow the understanding to come to you," M said. "It will. Want to go shopping?"

"I'm not much of a shopper."

"Oh, but this is your kind of shopping. How about a walk to collect a few pebbles for some special people—the healers who've prepared you to deliver your gift?"

"A rare good idea," I said.

"Thank you," M said.

As I walked, I thought about those who'd been there for me, working with me, preparing me—constant and loving and fun. For each of them, I picked up a small pebble from that place—the place so clearly shown in the painting, the place where this life magically connected to others, and the place where I performed the mysterious ceremony. It's a space and a moment in time I'll never forget.

What Goes Around
Comes Around

AFTER MY TRIP to Ireland, I entered what Serov called a *peaceful* time. It felt a lot like waiting.

While I waited, I changed. Some foods no longer agreed with me and I discovered I didn't need much to eat. I let go of dairy and grains. I almost let go of wine. I ate one meal a day—a lunch of fish or meat and vegetables—and sometimes a piece of fruit in the afternoon. I drank a lot of lemon ginger tea. For someone who loves to cook and eat, these changes were challenging, but I lost weight (a lot of it) and felt good. Walking, yoga, and an excess of stillness took over the empty spaces.

I rarely saw friends or family. I heard little from M and nothing from the others. One of the few things I noticed was a thought that popped in and out several times a day: *Be Here, Be Healthy, Be Love.* Otherwise, I received the occasional energetic nudge to pay attention to something, but that was about it. After a couple of months, I was growing weary of *peaceful* when I had this dream:

I'm climbing stairs in my house, going up to the attic.

I arrive at the attic door and notice light shining through the gap beneath it. I open the door and walk into the unfinished room— unpainted plywood walls and flooring. It's brightly lit. My eyes are having difficulty adjusting.

A kindly older man sits in a metal folding chair at a makeshift plywood desk on cinder blocks. He has white hair and a white beard. He's wearing khaki pants, a rumpled flannel shirt and an old-timey green eyeshade over his reading glasses. He's working on some papers, but turns to look at me over the top of his glasses.

"Come in, Steve," he says. "Light's bright, isn't it? Too bright sometimes. Had to put on this eyeshade. What brings you up here?"

"Thought I'd check in. Find out whether I'm doing what you wanted."

He smiles.

"You're doing fine. Is there anything I can help you with?"

"No. Not that I can think of."

"Great. Nice to see you."

He turns back to the papers on the desk and I walk back down the stairs.

When I woke up, M was laughing.

"I know, I know," I said. "Boots Mead is probably enjoying this."

"It just so happens he is," she said. "Fun, huh?"

"A hoot," I said. "A veritable laugh-a-minute."

"Speaking of Boots," M continued. "Remember your paper? The word *responsibility*? How you saw it differently and how it stuck with you?

"Sure," I said. "I've thought about it hundreds of times and tortured my children with it for years."

"It's been with you a good while. Why do you suppose that is?"

I remembered writing the seminar paper and, as I wrote, seeing the word *responsibility* clearly for the first time. I saw the word as two words, *response* and *ability*, and realized as my life unfolded, I had a choice. I could respond to things as I liked. No one controlled my choice. Whatever the circumstance, I was responsible for my response. I developed a mantra. It's the only one I've ever had.

Responsibility. The ability to respond. I can respond positively or negatively to things that happen in my life. It's my choice.

It helped me. I began to see life as a series of moments over which I often had little control, *except* for my response to them. No one could take that from me.

As my children grew up they too encountered the inevitable challenges of life. I heard a lot of *he said* or *she did this to me* or *they made me* or whatever and I'd say:

Responsibility. The ability to respond. You can respond positively or negatively to things that happen in your life. It's your choice.

As you might guess, this prompted a lot of eye-rolling but it was the only dad-saying I had, so I stuck with it and ultimately it stuck with them. One of my clever daughters, Abby, learned to use it against me.

"Dad, I had a little trouble with the car and it's going to cost a bundle to repair and remember what you always say, *Responsibility. The ability to respond. You can respond positively or negatively to things that happen in your life. It's your choice.*"

Abby smiled and high-fived her mother. (If you have a dad-saying, be prepared to live by it from time to time.)

Years later, Abby became an elementary school teacher and invited me to visit her classroom. There it was—my dad-saying—in big cardboard letters above the blackboard:

Responsibility. The ability to respond. You can respond positively or negatively to things that happen in your life. It's your choice.

I got goose bumps.

"For a good while now you've been talking about personal responsibility," M said. "The opportunity to choose love in every moment. It's your message and you've had a lot of practice delivering it."

"Easier said than done," I mused.

"So true and by the way, it's time to go again."

"Thank you Jesus."

"Exactly," M said.

"I've had enough peace to last me a while."

"So we noticed. Chomping at the bit to get on with things. You'll miss this time. Try to enjoy it."

"Okay, but I'm ready to go when it's time."

"It's time," M said. "Remember your other dream? The ladder? It shows the way."

"Sure," I said. "On the beach?"

"Yes," she said.

In the dream, I was standing precariously atop a very tall ladder—several stories tall. I was way up there, teetering on the ladder top, looking down at the beautiful white sandy beach far below. The ladder stood on the beach at the edge of the ocean. The water was clear, light blue and calm. Looking down, I wondered how I'd get down. The ladder felt unsteady and I feared I'd fall if I tried to go down. But I had to get down somehow. There wasn't anyone there to help me. So I screwed up my courage and stooped down carefully to put my hands on the ladder top and began to step down—facing away from the ladder rungs as I went. Gradually I felt more secure and knew I'd be fine. I descended slowly. Just a few ladder rungs above the beach, I woke up.

"What's it mean?" I asked.

"Let the meaning come to you. It shows the way ahead" M replied. "You know. You will see."

A few days later, I lay on Sandy's table. Serov showed up and said, "It's time for a meeting."

"A meeting?"

"Yes," Sandy said. "I heard that. It's time for a meeting."

"What meeting?" I asked.

As you might guess, there was no answer.

"Seriously unhelpful," I said. "He's left out the who-what-when-where-why-how. What am I supposed to do with that?"

"No doing," Sandy said. "Only allowing. Allow it to come to you."

Sandy was quiet for a while before saying, "I'm asked to tell you about my trip to Bhutan—one small part, but important for you. While there I visited places where Guru Rinpoche hid certain treasures in the Earth—treasures of wisdom that humans weren't ready to receive. Guru Rinpoche is a reincarnation of the Buddha and is called by many the Second Buddha."

I felt a sudden surge of energy—a strong nudge.

Sandy paused before continuing, "You might want to read about Guru Rinpoche and the treasures. I'm asked to give you my Druid wood and a small crystal I picked up near the cave where Guru Rinpoche hid several of the treasures. The energy of that place was powerful, Steve. You will carry the energy of Guru Rinpoche with you to the meeting."

I took the Druid wood and the small crystalline rock Sandy handed me. I could see the concern on her face again. She still didn't quite trust me with her Druid wood.

"Don't worry," I said. "I'll take good care of your treasures."

"I hear not to worry," she laughed. "I'll be with you at the meeting, I think. I'll keep a close eye on my treasures!"

A few days later I was on the table again—this time Ramona's table. She's a Reiki master, massage therapist and founder of the Nashville Center for Alternative Therapies. I have a weekly appointment with her.

"Where are you going?" she asked.

"Going?"

"I hear you're going somewhere. To a meeting. A healer is going to help you."

"We'll see," I said. "Maybe so. It's out of my hands. If it happens, I'll be there. I feel like I'm being called to the principal's office."

Two days later I lay on Jule's table. I told her about the meeting and the healer—the very little I knew.

"Chile," she said. "Patagonia? Are you going to Patagonia?"

"Not that I know of, but I've always wanted to. I looked at trips to Patagonia a couple of months ago. Felt pulled there for some reason. But nothing came of it. Didn't seem right for some reason."

"It wasn't the right time. Maybe it's time now."

"Okay. But where exactly? And when? And what's this about?"

"Don't know," Jule said. "I'm sure you'll know when you need to know."

"Jesus," I said.

And then, just a week later, I saw Bonnie. I told her about the meeting. Maybe in Chile. A healer there.

"That's interesting," Bonnie said. "A healer friend of mine emailed me yesterday. He lived here in Nashville for a lot of years and was one of my students just as you were. He's Chilean. His name is Nelson. He now lives in La Serena, a small town on the Chilean coast, where he grew up. I haven't heard from him in years. He emailed to ask if I was alright. Said he'd had a dream and was asked to contact me. He felt he needed to check in with me."

As she talked, energy flowed through me—a definite nudge.

"I'm getting goose bumps," Bonnie said. "Nelson's your healer."

"Yes, I think he is. Guess I'm going to Chile."

That evening, I emailed Nelson and several days later I booked my trip. On my 68th birthday, I'd be in La Serena with Nelson and attend the mysterious meeting. After the meeting, I'd fly to Patagonia and spend several days hiking in the Torres del Paine National Park, billed as the wildest place on Earth. It all fell into place effortlessly and it felt right.

When will I remember to let things come to me? I wondered.

"I've been wondering about that too," M said. "Maybe after your meeting you'll relax."

"What's the meeting about?" I asked.

"Perhaps you could let it come to you," M said gently. "Trust your knowing. The beauty will astound you. You are the healer. Never forget that. It's time. Remember what Shirley told you."

Shirley? I hadn't thought about Shirley in a very long time.

Over 10 years ago, Neal introduced me to a pet psychic named Shirley. She'd diagnosed an issue with one of the dogs that confounded our vet, so she came to me having already earned a bit of my trust.

"I have some things to share with you if you're open to hearing them," she said.

"Sure," I said warily.

At the time, I wasn't really open to much of anything, certainly not the prognostications of a psychic. But I was curious. I could listen. It wouldn't hurt to hear what she had to say.

"Good," she said. "I'll come to your office one day soon and we'll talk. It's best if I talk to you alone."

"Okay," I said, hesitating. "Why all the secrecy?"

"You'll understand when we talk."

A week or so later, Shirley met me in town.

"I have several messages for you," she started. "They come from my spiritual guides. Are you willing to hear them? You may find some of this unsettling."

How could I have said no at that point?

"I'm listening," I said.

"You're here at the farm for a short time—a few years more. It's a time of rest and recovery and an opening to your creativity. You'll soon write a book. It'll be a life review of sorts. The rest and remembering will open you to what comes next.

"Then you'll go. You'll move on. Neal will stay here—at least for a while. You'll know when it's time to go. Follow your heart. It'll all work out beautifully. You're opening to your purpose. You have a gift to deliver."

"A gift?"

"Yes," she said. "You'll step into a new life and deliver your gift. That's what I hear. You'll meet several healers. They'll help you find your way and prepare you to deliver your gift. One day you'll go to South America and you'll meet a great healer—a true shaman. He'll open a door for you and you'll step through it.

"Your new life is going to be magical. Follow your heart. There's nothing to fear. This is your time."

Shirley stopped talking. She sat looking at me.

There was a long silence before I said, "Is that it? I have a lot of questions…"

"And I have no answers," she laughed.

Amazing, I thought. *Shirley told me what was coming a long time ago and I promptly dismissed it all as fantasy. I soon forgot about it—the going, the gift, the healing. And now what she told me has happened, except for the part about the South American healer and delivering my gift. And now I'm going to Chile. I can't make this stuff up…*

Celebration

FEBRUARY IN SANTIAGO, Chile is hot and dry. When I arrived late morning, it was already 95 degrees.

I checked into a small hotel—Hotel Le Reve—where the staff were delightful and the courtyard was well-shaded by a large tree. After settling into my room and a short nap, I took a chair at a small table under the courtyard tree, ordered a cup of coffee and made some notes in my journal. The light breeze was refreshingly cool.

"Nice" M said.

"Yes it is."

"It's a gift to you—a place to rest before moving on. Enjoy and rest."

"I am."

"There's great joy for you among the Gathering. Your preparation is nearly complete. You'll soon be ready to deliver your gift—fully deliver your gift. We celebrate your preparation and what comes next for you. The road ahead is paved and you've got a new vehicle."

"Now that you mention it, I've been meaning to ask you about this new vehicle. Not much new I can see. It seems to have come with a bunch of used parts. My back is still giving me trouble."

M let that pass.

"Relax and enjoy every moment. Nelson will help open the door for you. You'll see the way ahead and step forward. In Patagonia, you begin fully delivering your gift. You bring healing to the Earth and uncover great treasures of wisdom for humankind."

"The treasures hidden by Guru Rinpoche? Sandy told me about them. I wondered why she told me. I had a feeling her story would be helpful somehow."

"Yes. The treasures. You begin to uncover them. You carry the energy of Guru Rinpoche."

"I do? I'm not aware of his energy."

"You embody his energy as you do the energies of your other lives. You will soon experience this. You will know."

For the next couple of days I walked in Santiago, soaking up the sun and sights and then, fully rested, I boarded a plane for La Serena.

⊷⟞⟝ ⟞⟝⟞⊶

A coastal town north of Santiago, La Serena is popular with vacation-ers escaping the heat of Chilean summer. A boardwalk punctuated with coffee shops, ceviche stalls, bike rental hawkers and amusement rides follows the broad, white-sand beach for several miles—perfect for strolling and people-watching.

"Hola," Nelson said, smiling broadly as we embraced.

"Hola," I said. I felt energy course through me as we hugged each other.

Nelson isn't a big man but has a captivating presence about him. Like most Chileans, he's dark-skinned and dark-eyed. His smile is broad and dimpled. He shaves his head and trims his beard short and neat. He says shaving reminds him every day who he is and what he does. He doesn't call himself a shaman, but he is. He has the presence and humil-ity of a great healer.

Over dinner we talked about our lives and how seemingly unlikely it was we'd come together at this time. I marveled at the parallels in our experiences. It was a homecoming of sorts—like catching up with a long-lost relative.

The next morning, Nelson picked me up at the hotel.

"Happy birthday," he said, smiling. "I think today you receive an unusual gift, Steve."

"Nelson, I've already received an unusual gift. I'm here with you."

"This morning has been interesting," he went on excitedly. "I've been feeling great waves of energy. Sometimes a heat comes. I can only describe it as a heat. It penetrates me and then goes away. I understand it as preparation for the ceremony I will perform with you this morning. I understand I've been preparing for this moment for a very long time. And now we are here to do this. It is part of a great mystery for me."

"And for me, Nelson. Whatever happens will be a surprise."

We arrived at Nelson's house. A modest 2-bedroom home in many ways like my own, it sits in a tranquil desert valley in the shadows of magnificent Andean peaks far from the busyness of La Serena. One of the bedrooms serves as Nelson's healing space. The healing table is surrounded by Nelson's musical instruments and gifts from his clients. The walls are covered with paintings and photographs collected over a lifetime. The space felt inviting and peaceful.

"You have music," Nelson said.

"Music…" I started, wondering what Nelson was talking about, but then I knew. "Yes, the music of Hildegard, another of my lives. I have some of her music on my phone."

"We will play her music for the first part of the ceremony."

I showed Nelson how to select the music he wanted to play and then lay on his table.

"You have some things for me?"

I retrieved Sandy's Druid wood, the Bhutanese crystal, and my clamshell from my pocket.

He placed the Druid wood in my left hand and the clamshell in my right hand. He put the crystal on my stomach just above my navel.

Energy began moving through me in an oblong circular pattern from my feet up the front of me to the top of my head and down my back returning to my feet, then surging upward again.

"And so we begin," Nelson said. "I hear it is time—time for a great celebration."

As he spoke, Hildegard's music played in the background. I felt a different energy begin to move through me from head to toe and suddenly I saw women gathering around me— M, Mother Mary, Grace, Sarah, Hildegard, a young woman with long, braided, raven-black hair I didn't know, Neal, Caroline, Sandy, Bonnie, Ramona, Jule, Coco, my Aunt Wiese, my grandmothers, my daughters, and so many more. The room was crowded with women, all around me.

"There are many women here," Nelson said. "Do you know them?"

"These are the women of my life." I felt tears coming. "They've participated in my preparation."

"Allow your arms to open and receive their love," Nelson said.

My arms lifted from the table and opened wide, exposing my heart. My hands turned palms up and opened—the Druid wood in my left hand, the clamshell in my right.

The energy shifted and began to course powerfully through me from left to right and right to left. Back and forth, I rocked as if I were on the deck of a rolling ship.

"A balancing," Nelson said. "Your male and female energies are clear and now you experience a balancing of those energies. It's time."

Gradually the strong movement of energy—left to right and right to left—shortened and quickened until suddenly the energy locked explosively into place, surged briefly, and calmed, flowing smoothly from head to toe in a line through the middle of my body.

"You're preparation is complete," Nelson announced and the room erupted in cheers and clapping.

My rising tears spilled over.

"Nelson, I've never felt this kind of love. It's overwhelming."

"I don't have words for this," he said. Nelson had tears in his eyes too. "I've never experienced anything like this, Steve. Your male and female energies are now balanced—as closely as they can be in this life. You embody a strong, well-balanced male energy, but the new energy you now bring in fullness to the Earth requires that you have feminine support. You have a feminine partner though you may not always be aware of her. Let this understanding come to you. You've had much help from the women who've nurtured you and they continue to support you as you will soon see. They are with you. Always with you. You are never alone."

Nelson paused before going on. The energy in the room calmed and the women, quietly waving goodbye, faded away. I moved my arms back to my sides on the table and Nelson turned off the music.

"Now you go on a shamanic journey," he said. "This will not be anything like what you might expect. Let go of expectations. Simply let this unfold for you as it will. You are shown what comes next. A door opens for you."

As I lay on the table, Nelson played an instrument that sounded much like a didgeridoo. Deep guttural sounds bounced around the room and suddenly I was as a child turning over moss-covered stones in a stream on the wooded hillside across the street from the house where I grew up. The scene shifted and I was a young boy wading the edge of a pond on my uncle's farm under a hot sun. Next I was a young man fly-fishing on a Montana river—my favorite place on the planet. Then I was a middle-aged father lying on my back on the ground under brilliant stars on the vast salt flats of the Makgadikgadi Pan in Botswana. The scene shifted one last time and I sat in a patio chair as a 68 year-old grandfather in the small garden behind my house, watching a pair of cardinals hop branch to branch in the purple plum tree nearby.

Shifting scenes came quickly now as I revisited the other seven lives I've told you about. In each, I saw myself walking a path and I understood walking as a thread that runs through my many lives on this Earth.

"Like the women of your life, the Earth has nurtured you. She has supported you," Nelson said. "And now you go to walk the Earth once again. You bring the Earth your gift—the renewing energy you carry. You will walk in many places and infuse the new energy into the Earth. The first of these places is Patagonia. Other places will follow. You will know where and when and with whom. Trust your knowing. Do not allow others to deter you. You will know and you will go."

The energy subsided again and all was quiet. Nelson allowed the silence to surround us for a minute or so and then sounded a single soft tone on one of his instruments. It sounded like a small bell of some sort.

The ceremony was over.

I lay on the table feeling very tired. Nelson was tired too.

"Happy birthday," M said.

"Quite the party," I said.

"Yes it was," Nelson nodded.

"A little something out of the ordinary," M said. "And now it's time for a rest. Listen to your body. Take the next couple of days and recover before Patagonia. Allow the events of this day to settle. Trust your knowing. You know and after a brief rest, as Nelson said, you will walk the Earth again."

⋅→═◉ ◉═←⋅

That night, after sleeping away most of the day, I met Nelson and his friend, Ingrid, for dinner.

Ingrid was born in Germany and grew up there, but over a lifetime found her way to La Serena. She and Nelson have been healing partners for years, much as Caroline and I have been partners. I'd asked Nelson whether I'd have the chance to meet Ingrid and he planned dinner with her after the ceremony.

When I saw Ingrid I realized I somehow knew her. She wore a white skirt and blouse and a sweet smile. We hugged like old friends.

"I feel like I know you," I said.

Ingrid smiled again.

"You do," she said. "We are old friends."

Over dinner, she explained that she and I were, in prior lives, young Mayan girls in the Yucatan and best friends around 350 AD. She went on to say that she remembered my having long braided dark hair.

"The young girl I saw today during the ceremony. I didn't know who she was…"

"Yes," Ingrid said excitedly. "I call her Maya. She wants you to know she is with you now and will go with you to Patagonia to participate in the ceremony you perform there."

As Ingrid spoke, a delightful, youthful energy moved in close to me and I felt Maya at my left shoulder.

"I feel Maya here now," I said. "She's the last of the eight soul connections needed to support me and she arrives just before I go to Patagonia. This is extraordinary."

"Yes, Steve. Maya is here and so very happy," Ingrid said. "She is one of the feminine energies traveling with you to Patagonia. I am here for your reunion with Maya. I am so delighted."

"And I'm delighted to have met you, Ingrid. Thank you both. What a day we've had. I'll never forget this."

After dinner, I fell back into bed. For the next two days, I napped, walked between naps, and ate meals with Nelson between walks. He was resting too. Over a lunch of freshly-caught fish the day before my onward trip to Patagonia, Nelson produced a map of the world. He asked me to mark the places I'd visited to connect with other lives and suggested I do the same when I returned home to Nashville.

"We will soon see a pattern in your travels. It's a new energy grid you create around the Earth and beyond. It may look two dimensional but I'm told it's multi-dimensional and beyond our human understanding. It will benefit the Earth and all her creatures. This is your path."

I marked spots on the map and handed it back to Nelson.

"Thank you, Nelson, for this and all you've done. I'm eternally grateful."

"Me too, Steve. It's been a magical time for me. I hope we'll keep up."

"I'd like that. I'm sure we will."

Blue Towers

THE NEXT DAY, I was off to Chile's nether region—the place called Patagonia. After a four-hour flight to the seaport of Punta Arenas and a four-hour shuttle ride from there into the wilderness, I arrived at Explora Patagonia Hotel. It's in the middle of nowhere.

Perched above a crystalline blue lake with stunning views of rugged snow-capped mountains called the Torres del Paine (blue towers), the hotel reminds me of a cruise ship moored in a wonderfully wild setting. When I arrived, clouds swirled around the mountain summits and gusty winds ripped across the lake whipping up whitecaps.

It was a place to fall into the natural rhythm of things—an early morning walk along the lakeshore before breakfast, a day hike with interesting people and capable guides, a hot shower, and some downtime before dinner and a good night's sleep.

"Enjoy," M said. "This is yet another gift to you. You remember how to receive."

"I could get into receiving like this."

"Receive and give. It's a beautiful dance. Soon you will give a small portion of the gift you bring. The experience of this giving will be powerful. Enjoy your hiking, but take time to relax and rest. And have some fun."

"I am. This is my kind of camping."

M laughed. "You'll have many opportunities to go camping. This is good practice."

"I'm pretty sure I have a talent for this. This could be another of the few things I do well."

"You have a beautiful talent for this."

⊶ ⊷

I was traveling solo…

"You never travel solo," M said.

Well, okay, but I felt like I was traveling solo much of the trip which opened me to meeting other people during the day's hike or over a glass of wine before dinner. Every night I ate dinner with somebody new. I enjoyed people from all over—Australia, Scotland, Japan, Canada, China, Peru, Argentina, and Brazil—even some fellow Tennesseans. I began to see solo travel as a way of exploring new places and new people—not better or worse than traveling with friends or family, just different and in so many ways enlivening.

"You meet people now who'll help you," M went on. "Be open and receive. Pay attention to what you hear from them. Many come to you now who are messengers. This is a time of noticing. Traveling solo, as you see it, opens you to receiving these gifts. So many gifts."

For the next couple of days, I enjoyed my newfound rhythm. The wilderness renewed me. Even my brain relaxed—a rare thing for sure. There was nothing holding me to the past and no need to think ahead. Being there was more than enough—open, spacious and free. I loved it. I hiked, ate too much, met fascinating people and slept like a baby until the morning of the fourth day when I woke unusually early.

I lay in bed looking out the window. The sky was clear and full of stars—starlight so bright the outline of the mountains above the lake showed itself as a glowing jagged line.

And I knew.

Time for a ceremony, I thought. *Time to go…*

I got out of bed. I was the only person up. The hotel was otherwise quiet. I dressed and retrieved Sandy's Druid wood, the Bhutanese crystal, my clamshell and a small white stone I'd found at the edge of a glacial lake on a hike—a small piece of Patagonia. I put these things in my pocket and wandered out into the starlit night.

It was surprisingly warm out. A light breeze came and went. There was just enough starlight to find my way along a path to the top of a small featureless hill several hundred yards from the hotel. Standing atop the hill, I knew it was the place I'd heard about—the place where the mountains come down to the water—and I knew what to do. I stooped to place the four talismans in a pattern on the ground at my feet and stood up.

As I did a gust of wind came off the lake and knocked me backwards several steps before I regained my balance. The wind was unexpected and it kept coming. I waded into it to stand above the talisman pattern on the ground and again the wind knocked me backward a few steps.

Hmmm, I thought. *Maybe I'm not supposed to stand...*

"Step up," Serov said through the raging wind. "Trust your knowing."

So I stepped up to the spot where I'd stood twice before and leaned heavily into the wind. I felt Sandy, Maya and Ingrid at my left shoulder. Their energies were comforting.

This is like something out of a movie, I thought.

"What's your intention?" M asked softly.

These are the words that came out of me—they did not feel like my words:

"For the Earth, for humankind, for the All," I said into the staggering wind.

At that, a cloud of energy surged and swirled above me, struck the top of my head, barreled through me into the Earth at my feet and exploded around me in every direction—a powerful explosion. I'd never felt anything like it. It came fiercely through me for a few seconds without resistance and then, as quickly as it had come, it subsided. The wind dropped to a light breeze and I stood motionless atop the hill while my body vibrated.

Wow, I thought. *That was something...*

All was quiet around me. The energy circulating in my body slowed and I noticed sunlight grazing the summits of the mountains above the lake. A few lights were on in the hotel. The place was waking up.

It's done, I thought. *The ceremony is done. That was something...*

I waited to see if Serov or M had anything more to say.

As you might guess, they didn't.

Alright then, it's time for breakfast...

I picked up the four objects at my feet, put them in my pocket and walked back to the hotel. Inside, I started toward the dining room but suddenly felt the exhaustion I'd felt after my right of passage with Nelson.

Maybe a short nap before breakfast...

I headed for my room where I fell face down on the bed. I slept all day, woke up in time for dinner, ate a little bit, and went back to bed.

The next day I was fine. I had plenty of energy and enjoyed a strenuous day of hiking—my last full day in the rhythm.

Early the following morning before my long ride back to civilization, I walked to the top of the hill where I'd performed the ceremony to take one last look. Billowing clouds shrouded the mountain summits and reflected their grayness on the lake surface below. A light breeze swept across the lake and up the hill to me.

For the Earth, for humankind, for the All, I thought.

"That seems to cover it," M said. "Quite the adventure, isn't it?"

"Yes, it is. I'll miss this place."

"Soak it up and let go. You have other places to walk."

"I hope they're all places like this. I like the wild places."

"Let this come to you and remember to pay attention. Messengers come to you now more quickly than you might imagine. It's time," M said.

She paused.

"Have you thought more about your dream?" she went on. "Stepping down the ladder?"

"No, I haven't."

"The meaning of the dream has come to you. You embody its meaning now. There was only one way down the ladder and it was important that you stepped down noticing each ladder rung—paying attention—to find your way. It's the reason Serov and Sarah have been encouraging you to *step forward slowly*. Stepping forward slowly, allowing the way to be shown to you, you have found your way to this place.

"You stand where mountain meets water—where your masculine energy meets its feminine counterpart standing beside you. In the intertwining of male and female, the new energy finds its fullness. It's the balance struck on Nelson's table and fulfilled in this place. Do you see?"

I did see. The understanding was now part of me—part of my *knowing*.

"Thank you," I said.

"You never walk alone. Rest in this understanding. Your feminine partners walk with you—always with you."

Stepping Forward

AFTER BREAKFAST, I boarded a hotel van back to Punta Arenas. A couple sat on the bench seat in front of me. They were from Australia—Bert and Margaret.

"I've never been to your part of the world," I said, making small talk. "Maybe I'll get there one of these days."

I felt an energetic nudge.

"Australia's a big place," Margaret said. "Lots to see. Perhaps your next trip?"

Another nudge...

"Where would you suggest I go?"

"Our favorite is Tasmania. We love Tasmania. Bert and I have been several times. My favorite bit is the area around Lake St. Clair."

"Mine too," said Bert. "A wild place. It feels a little like Patagonia."

While they talked, energy moved through me—encouraging me to pay attention.

Next stop Tasmania, I thought. *Lake St. Clair...*

"Good," Sarah said. "Enjoy yo' walk, child. Up dat hill and 'roun da bend..."

"To Lake St. Clair," Grace added, laughing.

That was quick, I thought.

Back in Nashville, I lay on Sandy's table telling her more than she probably wanted to know about my trip. When I mentioned I'd felt her presence on Nelson's table and again at the ceremony in Patagonia, she said she'd felt the energies of those events but hadn't been conscious of what was happening. (Ingrid has since told me the same thing.)

"I knew something was happening with you," Sandy said. "It's all quite amazing, Steve. I know I travel with you somehow—first Ireland and now Patagonia. And I know your energy traveled with me to Bhutan. But I'm not sure how I participate or how others are involved. I hear now you go somewhere else—another place."

"Yes," I said. "Tasmania. Lake St. Clair. I'm going in June."

Sandy smiled, "Your friend Grace must be very happy. And how quickly that came to you."

"Things seem to be speeding up and I'm okay with it."

"More than okay with it," M said. "Always itching to go."

A few minutes later, Sandy said, "And now I hear you go somewhere after Tasmania."

"I think you might be right."

"I hear you *know*."

Now I smiled. "I'll go to Scotland in the fall. Edinburgh and the Outer Hebrides. To a village called Callanish. A couple of years ago, I painted a landscape with mountains in the distance—mountains locals call *The Sleeping Beauty of the Moors*. I wondered whether I'd go there someday. Now I know."

"Maybe my Druid wood will travel with you."

I felt Sandy tense.

"I won't lose your Druid wood," I said.

Down Under

"SHE'LL MAKE HERSELF available," M said.

Australia was on my calendar. I'd be trekking in Tasmania's mountainous middle, wandering its Freycinet Peninsula, and circumambulating Australia's big red rock, Uluru.

Walking, walking, walking.

I wondered whether I'd be performing a ceremony in Australia like the one in Patagonia. If so, where? What would it look like? I was new at this. Would I have a female partner as I had in Patagonia? Would she be there like Ingrid and Maya and Sandy? Energetically or for real? If a real person, where would I meet her? My mind churned.

"She'll make herself available while you're there," M said again.

"Who's *she*?"

No answer.

"Okay," I said, trying to tease out a response, "just so you know, I'm flying blind here. You might want to toss me a bone. Share a bit of your vast perspective."

It didn't work.

Jesus, I thought. *More waiting. More allowing. More letting things come...*

"God got da pen, child," Sarah said.

⊶═◉ ◉═⊷

Sydney is a sparkling-clean, beautiful city. It reminds me of Seattle. It's friendly, bustling, and blustery. Its iconic Opera House – the one you see on the postcards—hovers over a busy harbor. For three days I explored Sydney while my body processed 15 hours of time difference. I slept when I was sleepy, ate when I was hungry and walked when I wasn't sleeping or eating. On more than one occasion, generally after long ambles through the Royal Botanical Gardens just a few blocks from the hotel, I relaxed at one of the open-air eateries lining the harbor front, sampling Australian wines and soaking up the view. The sunsets were breathtaking.

"Welcome to Australia," M said.

On the morning of my last day in Sydney, I had time for a walk before flying on to Tasmania. It was a Seattle-kind-of-day. The skies were gray and spitting rain. Clouds skirted the tops of gleaming-glass skyscrapers and ubiquitous construction cranes. Fleeting sunbreaks illuminated wet sidewalks. Umbrellas jostled for space above the heads of commuters who juggled the umbrellas and their coffee cups. The laid-back Aussies of lore were moving fast.

I kept pace—mostly because I had no choice in the matter—till I wandered onto a block-long street out of the busyness where I heard the faint sound of bagpipes.

Interesting, I thought. *My next trip is Scotland. Wonder…*

I felt an energetic nudge.

Hmmm…well…alright…

The short street emptied onto an open plaza where a lone bagpiper in full kit— cap, jacket, kilt, purse, knee socks and heavy boots—stood stock-straight in the mist playing a melancholy tune. I walked toward him, smiled, put a few Aussie dollars in the basket at his feet, nodded my thanks and walked on, thinking *Maybe I'm supposed to talk to him.*

Another energetic nudge.

That's ridiculous. Talk to him. About what? He's busy…

Another energetic nudge.

You've got to be kidding…

Yet another nudge.

That's the way it went for several blocks, before I stopped in the middle of the crowded sidewalk, bucked the advancing umbrellas, flapped my arms like a penguin and said aloud, "Okay, I'll go talk to him."

Folks looked at me like I was nuts which I temporarily was.

Back at the plaza, a small group of 5 or 6 people stood around the bagpiper listening.

Again, I thought *I shouldn't interrupt...*

Another energetic nudge and the bagpiper's small audience dispersed. I no longer had an excuse to avoid him, so I walked up and stood listening till he stopped playing.

"Can I help you with something?" he asked.

"Well, I believe you can but I have no earthly idea what that might be. Are you from Scotland?"

"No. I'm Australian, but went to university there. That's where I picked up the bagpipes."

"Hmm," I said. "I'm going to Scotland in a couple of months. Where would you suggest I go? Some place you liked..."

He didn't hesitate, "Pitlochry. My favorite. Are you going to Edinburgh?"

Strong energetic nudge.

"I'll be in Edinburgh for several days..."

"Good. Go to Pitlochry. It's a short train ride. Spend the day. You won't regret it. Wonderful walking in the hills around the village. There's a beautiful river. Can't remember the name of it, but it's been dammed into a stretch of lakes. Gorgeous. And some nice restaurants. Good lunch spots on the water if you want to do a picnic. I'd love to go back."

Another nudge.

"Nice," I said. "Guess I'm going to Pitlochry. Many thanks."

"Wish I were going with you."

I nodded and he resumed playing. As I wandered away, encouraging energy buzzed through me.

"Paying attention," M said. "Doing your part, asking others for help, allowing the universe to do the rest. A good thing to remember."

"Mo' heppers comin', child. Let 'em do," Sarah added.

Lord, I thought, *I just got to Australia and already I'm pointed to a place in Scotland. I can't make this stuff up...*

"One more thing," M said. "When you book your train to Pitlochry, you might want to buy two tickets."

"One for me. And one for?"

It was a wasted question. I knew it when I asked.

"Well, just to be clear, I hope it's a her—a real her, I mean. Energetic companions are nice and all but...well...you know what I'm saying... and as long as I'm hoping, I hope she has a nice little bottom."

"And a kind heart. Surely she should have a kind heart," M added.

"Sure..."

"And a fertile mind. You'd want that. And a playful sense of humor. And an adventurous spirit. And a creative bent. Someone who loves to walk. Someone who'll patiently listen to your endless stories. And..."

"Yes. All that. So what do you think?"

There was laughter – lots of laugher. It went on a bit too long if you want my opinion.

⋅⊱═⊙ ⊙═⊰⋅

I flew to Hobart, Tasmania later that afternoon and checked into a delightful little hotel. They'd saved me a comfortable room on Hobart's quiet harbor. After I settled in, I ventured out to inspect the place.

I was hungry.

I should wait till dinner, I thought as I strolled by an authentic-looking seafood shack—authentic-looking mostly because it looked like it was falling down.

Something smelled good.

I should wait...
Oh, what the hell...
Giving my better judgment a rest, I ate the fish and chips.
They were amazing.
I didn't know it before I arrived, but an arts festival –Dark Mofo—
was in the works and I'd caught its leading edge. As the sun went down,
I noticed a series of festively lit, towering red crosses lining the pedes-
trian walkway across the harbor.
A chill ran down my spine. *Lord*, I thought. *What's that about?*
"A little reminder," M said. "Rivers of blood have been spilled in
your name."
She paused to let that sink in.
"You'll be asked about that life and the others," she went on.
"I can't answer questions. I feel the energies of those lives, but I
have no memory of them."
"You've been spared the memories. If you had the memories, your
responses would contradict what's written and what's believed. Imagine
the controversy – the swirl. This life's not about correcting the record.
Let the old stories be. It's time to move on. Live the story of this life. It's
quite a story. Live it and tell it. When you're questioned about your other
lives, be grateful for your poor memory."

→═◎ ◎═←

I requested a small, eco-compact car for the drive to Lake St. Clair. I was
the only passenger and had almost no luggage. Standing at the counter
in the car rental office, a tiny car that barely gripped the road seemed a
sensible choice. There were several big honking 4x4's with heavy duty
tires available, but I missed their message. I probably should have asked
a few questions when the rental car guy pushed hard on the extra auto
repair insurance.

"Most people get it," he said.

I declined the insurance, blithely signed all the papers he piled up in front of me, grabbed the key and headed for the car.

"Other side," the rental car guy yelled from his office.

"What?"

"The driver's seat is on the other side."

"Oh. Sorry. Right. Thanks."

It was not an auspicious beginning.

Driving on the wrong side of the road required every ounce of my attention for the first few miles, but I found my way out of Hobart and entered another world—a fairy tale.

I drove through vast valleys patchworked in brilliant hues of green and yellow. Clearwater creeks meandered through lush meadows. There were dark forests of unfamiliar trees living in the shadows of snow-capped mountains. The air was fresh, even crisp, and full of enticing smells.

Wallabies and wombats were everywhere. Some unfortunate number of them had not quite made it across the road.

Shoulda gotten the insurance, I thought.

The mountainous middle of Tasmania is sparsely populated. The neighbors are a long way away. I rarely saw another vehicle and when I did it was a big honking 4x4 with heavy duty tires, often equipped with an air-intake extension over the roof.

Hmmm, I thought. *Probably a reason...*

As I processed that thought, the pavement under my eco-compact gave way to gravel. Fifteen minutes further on, gravel gave way to red dirt. Instantly, red dirt gave way to potholes.

Jeepers, I thought.

The last several miles to Lake St. Clair were daunting, but my eco-compact and I arrived without incident. Both of us sighed. Why the tires weren't flat, I don't know. I sat looking out the car window across the lake. The wildness of the place was jaw-dropping. I loved it.

Lake St. Clair is deep, cold, and pristine. It feeds on snowmelt and, in turn, nourishes everything around it. The views across the lake are expansive and constantly changing. The view from my room reminded me of Patagonia. I could see why I'd been led to this place. While I admired the view, a family of platypuses played at the lake's edge just below my window.

I've always wanted to see one of those, I thought.

Over the next 3 days, I walked the lakeshore, hiked to other, smaller mountain lakes and ate family-style with travelers from all over. Many were Australian and most of them were visiting Tasmania for the first time. It turns out Tasmania is a long way from everywhere, including the mothership. Aside from meals, I rarely saw another human being.

Late one morning, after a particularly rigorous hike, I took an unscheduled nap. When I woke, Grace spoke up.

"What do you think?"

"I love this place."

"Want to take a short walk before lunch?"

"Sure. Are you coming?"

"Most of the way. You might want to bring your trinkets."

I'd packed my clamshell, Sandy's Druid wood, a small Buddha statue Sandy was encouraged to send with me, and a slender quartz crystal from Brazil. It seemed like a lot of stuff—too much really—but I dutifully stuffed the stuff into my jacket pocket and we were off. That makes it sound like we were moving quickly, but we weren't. I stopped every few steps to admire another rock – so many and so different from anything I'd ever seen.

Grace led me, in fits and starts, around the lakeshore to a spot not far from the hotel. Little waves lapped lazily at the rocky beach. The sky was full of noontime sun. A few small clouds hung around the mountain peaks in the distance. A lone platypus swam by.

"Probably the dad," I said, admiring a slick red pebble.

"Where mountain meets water," Grace reminded me.

"Right. Time for a ceremony? I was wondering when we'd get around to this."

I prepared myself for an experience like the one in Patagonia. I arranged the four talismans in what seemed an appropriate pattern on a large rock at the water's edge and added the slick red pebble to the pattern.

Look at all that stuff. This is gonna be some ceremony...

Without fanfare, Sandy's energy arrived comfortably at my left side.

"Nice. You're here."

"Yes," she said.

Extraordinary, I thought. *I'm talking to Sandy's energy and she's talking back. How does...*

I felt energy stirring lightly in me and noticed Sandy's energy moving closer. Our energies languidly intertwined and slowly expanded around us.

The words *trust you knowing* rang in my ears.

"Okay, let's do this," I said, mostly to myself.

I stood above the talismans, looked out across the lake, and extended my arms palms out. I braced myself for big winds and powerful bolts of lightning, then said aloud, "For the Earth, for humankind, for the All."

I felt the gently intertwining energies surge briefly and release, moving smoothly across the lake for a few seconds.

That was it.

The ceremony was over.

No gale-force winds, lightning bolts, or deafening thunder. No voices ringing from the heavens. No choir singing Alleluias. Sandy's energy was there briefly and gone without a goodbye. The whole thing felt insubstantial. It wasn't what I expected.

"I traveled all the way to Australia for that?" I said.

"Just what's needed," M said. "No more, no less."

She let that settle.

"Some time ago, you asked for a message – one just for you. Well, here's one. Your partnership with Sandy is special. It's extraordinary. Honor it. Together you bring healing to the Earth."

"Sandy's my partner? How can..."

"She was with you in Ireland. You traveled with her in Bhutan. She accompanied you to Patagonia. And now she makes herself available here."

"*She'll make herself available.* That's what you meant..."

"Yes."

"So, we're sort of energetic partners sometimes."

"Not sort of. When needed, your energies entwine with Sandy's to create a third energy—a divine energy that renews the Earth. The ceremonies, as you describe them, are blessings – Earth blessings. You walk with Sandy now as partners and every step you take together is a blessing. Some you will experience more powerfully than others. Your experiences of them will vary, but they are all blessings and they are just what's needed."

"This is otherworldly," I said.

M was quiet while I gathered the talismans and returned them to my pocket.

"Much lies ahead," she said. "Let the experiences of your partnership come to you."

When I got back to my room I sent Sandy a message saying I'd performed a blessing at noon Australia time (9pm Nashville time the night before). I said her energy had shown up for it. When I heard back, she said she'd felt her energy move away briefly about that time. It felt peaceful and easy and all happened quickly. She'd wondered whether I was performing a ceremony.

"Yes," I responded. "That's just the way it was."

⤙══◎ ◎══⤚

Steve Johnson

A few days later, I was headed to Wineglass Bay on Tasmania's Freycinet Peninsula— one of the top 10 most beautiful beaches on the planet according to the folks who rank such things. I was looking at a 4-hour drive if conditions were good *and* I was driving a big honking 4x4 with heavy duty tires. But I wasn't. So my eco-compact and I settled for a 6-hour trip on a longer, mostly paved, route.

Oh bother, I thought.

Not surprisingly, annoyance quickly gave way to wonder. The drive was delightful. The landscape was magical. So were the signs. Along the way, I bypassed the town of Jericho, crossed over the Jordan River and topped St. Patrick's Pass.

"You're welcome," M said.

The Freycinet Peninsula juts into the Pacific Ocean halfway along Tasmania's east coast. It's mostly mountains – not especially tall ones, but mountains nonetheless –and their flanks fall precipitously into the sea.

Where mountain meets water, I thought. *Here we go...*

While I knew I was traveling to Australia to perform Earth blessings, I had no idea how many or exactly where. After my visit to Lake St. Clair, I was simply going where my heart wanted to go and first on its list was a beach – a nice remote uncrowded one.

"Wineglass Bay," the hotel clerk said. "Yes. A must-see. It's a bit of a hike, but it's worth it."

"It's on every travel magazine list I've seen. Is it crowded?"

"Go early," she said. "It's winter here. You'll have the place to yourself."

I can occasionally take direction – particularly if it's to avoid crowds. The next morning I pulled on my hiking boots in the dark.

"You might want to take your clamshell and Sandy's Druid wood," M said.

"What about the other stuff? The Buddha and the …"

"You won't need them."

"Good," I said.

I showed up at the Wineglass Bay trailhead before sun-up. Dawn was creeping across the sky. It promised to be a beautiful day, cool but sunny – a perfect day for hiking and walking a beach. Nobody else was there. I was, as far as I could tell, the only intruder and in that quietly majestic place, I felt like one.

The hike over the steep mountain pass down to the bay is enough to keep some folks away. The ascent was heart-pounding and the descent thigh-burning, but the effort was absolutely worthwhile. After an hour of climbing, I stepped onto the most beautiful beach I've ever seen – all alone. A great expanse of fine white sand stretched for a half mile or so in a broad arc around a small bay partly shaded from the sun by the mountain I'd just clambered over.

It's a good thing the mountain's there, I thought. *Otherwise, the place would be chock-a-block in condos.*

Huge boulders anchored one end of the beach. They were pock-marked and studded with small pools of exceedingly clear, frigidly cold water deposited overnight by the surf.

"Perhaps you'd like to bathe your clamshell and Sandy's Druid wood in one of the pools," M said.

"Okay. Sure."

I did as M suggested and stood back. Sandy's Druid wood floated quietly above my less-than-buoyant clamshell. Except for the rhythm of waves marking time, all was peaceful.

Time for a blessing, I thought.

I knew what to do.

I retrieved the Druid wood and clamshell from their bath. I held Sandy's Druid wood in my left hand and the clamshell in my right and extended my arms toward the horizon, palms up.

Instantly Sandy's energy was there next to me – at my left side – but this time powerfully so. Her energy filled the air around me and our energies intertwined quickly and intensely, twisting far into the sky above my head.

"For the Earth, for humankind, for the All," I said aloud, and the swirling energies rushed through me powerfully into the Earth and across the sea to the horizon. Every cell of my body luxuriated in the flow.

"That's more like it," I said.

Sandy laughed.

"Awesome," she said.

This time Sandy's energy stayed. We walked down the beach together as if she were actually there, talking about the beauty of the place, the awesome ceremony, and the mystery of our partnership. We laughed a lot, until…

She was gone.

Talking to Sandy's energy. Imagine that…

The next day, Sandy emailed that she'd felt the blessing's power and had to sit down, rest for a couple of hours, and eat *a lot*, before she recovered.

It was now clear to both of us we were energetic partners in some quite amazing way. We knew what M had told us and what we'd each experienced, but little more.

"Much lies ahead," M said.

⋆⊨◎ ◎⊨⋆

There's more I'd like to write about Tasmania – the Friendly Beaches where I walked for half a day and never saw another person, the Freycinet Marine Farm where I ate some delicious steamed prawns, the nice young couple at Geographe Restaurant in Coles Bay, Hobart's Saturday Market, and the mind-bending art collection at MONA – but time to move on. I loved Tasmania and I miss my eco-compact car. It was impractically cute.

From Hobart, I flew nearly 2000 miles back through Sydney and on to Uluru—the big red rock in the middle of Australia's outback which, even in the dead of Aussie winter, can be a hot place. I stayed in tent-like accommodations that offered no actual *camping out* experience but did offer incredible views of cloudless skies, endless desert and the big rock.

As remote and hot as the place is, and in spite of annoying desert flies, Uluru is popular with tourists. It drew me in like it had the indigenous peoples, the Anangu, millennia ago.

The Anangu now manage the area around Uluru. The rock and its surroundings are sacred to them. Though I walked around the big red rock and spent a day hiking through the smaller, but still massive red rocks of Kata Tjuta nearby, I was not asked to perform Earth blessings there and glad of it. The places felt holy to me and well-tended. Sometimes helping isn't.

I haven't written about this till now, but off and on during the trip, I struggled with loneliness—the dark side of solo travel. I often enjoy being alone. Sometimes I crave it. And yes, I know I'm never really alone. My ethereal helpers are always here. When I choose, I can hike with real people or share a meal with them. But I occasionally long for a companion and it gets me down.

After a morning walk around Uluru and a light lunch, I retreated to my air-conditioned room and relaxed into a comfortable chair gazing at the vast desert outside and the big red rock in the distance.

I was lonely.

The big rock looked lonely too—out there all by itself, eternally alone.

I don't know where the tears came from, but they came and I wept.

"Let dis go child," Sarah said, trying to comfort me. "Jus' let 'em go."

"I know, but…"

"I'm here," Sandy said quietly. Her energy was back at my side – light, easy, comfortable. I felt her take my left hand and hold it. Her touch was soothing. I felt the loneliness lifting.

"How about some music?" M suggested. "To lighten you up."

"Yes," Sandy agreed.

I found a playlist on my phone, punched *shuffle* and put the phone down. Elton John began singing *Can You Feel the Love Tonight*.

Sandy laughed. "I like to dance," she said.

Sure, but how..."

She took my hand again and I got up. I held her as if she were really there and we danced. Oh how we danced. Effortlessly. Gliding easily around the room. Sandy sometimes twirling away and coming back. Holding and letting go. It was delightful.

"We're really doing this," I marveled.

Sandy smiled. "Look," she said.

As we danced, our energies expanded – building slowly and inter-lacing. The more we danced, the faster the energies began to swirl. My body tingled all over.

"Let's do this," Sandy said excitedly, and without another word between us, we turned to face the open desert and the big rock. Standing side-by-side, we held hands and extended our free hands to the horizon, palms open to the sky, and the energies surged through us, moving in towering waves across the desert to the horizon. The feeling of it was explosive – utterly explosive. We stood for a minute or so in the afterglow and watched the renewing energies settle on the Earth around us as far as we could see.

"Want to do that again?" I asked, only half joking.

Sandy laughed.

"Awesome!" she said and was gone.

Several hours later, I received a message from her asking if I'd per-formed another blessing. She said she'd again felt her energy leave and some minutes later, return. She felt exhausted and was having to rest.

"Yes," I responded. "Too much to capture in an email. I'll tell you all about it when I get back. But thanks. You're good company."

Several days later, I was headed home.

Somewhere high over the Pacific Ocean, M said, "Walking in partnership with the feminine, you have a better understanding of your gift and the healing you and your partner bring to the Earth. You and Sandy have a lot to talk about. Rest now. Soon you walk again. You never walk alone."

Revelations

HOME AGAIN, I lay on Sandy's table receiving some much-needed help with wearying jet lag and a neck complaining bitterly about 30 hours of non-stop travel. Re-entry was challenging, plus I'd developed a cold.

"Now maybe you'll rest," Sandy suggested.

"Or you could use your mysterious powers and fix all this today."

She laughed.

"Or maybe now you'll rest."

We talked about Sydney and bagpipes, Tasmania, Uluru, Earth blessings, energetic partnerships, and tight hamstrings. I returned her Druid wood and her Buddha. We were back to our real lives and our every-other-week appointment schedule.

"When is Scotland?" Sandy asked.

"Two months from now. Toward the end of August."

"You'll do Earth blessings there?"

"I think so. In Pitlochry and somewhere near Callanish, if I had to guess. I'll know when I get there."

"Maybe my Druid wood will go with you."

"Maybe so. I'm sure we'll know when we get closer to the trip. I have a feeling something is getting ready to change."

"What change?"

"I don't know. It's just a feeling. Like we're turning a page. Like God's writing a new chapter. I've heard he has the pen now."

A few nights later I had dinner with a friend who's an Episcopal priest and excessively well-read. I told him about Australia, the Earth blessings and my surprising energetic partnership with Sandy.

"*Hieros gamos,*" he said. "That's Greek. In English, it's *sacred marriage.* I've never seen it but I've read about it. It's quite rare. You might want to look it up."

Several days later, I saw Bonnie. In the course of updating her, I mentioned *hieros gamos.*

"Yes," she said. "It's the partnership you and Sandy have. Normally it grows from the seed of a physical relationship, but you and Sandy don't seem to need that connection. Your preparation has been extensive. I've been here for most of it. I'm guessing Sandy's been preparing for this all her life too. It's beautiful, Steve. The intertwining of divine masculine and feminine energies to nourish the Earth. It's what you do and it fits with your dream—your vision of the Earth a thousand years from now."

And then I caught up with Nelson. He wanted to know about my trip and the ceremonies. I brought up *hieros gamos.*

"Ah," he said. "Yes, Steve. I see. That is the nature of your partnership with Sandy. When I was an art professor years ago, I studied the art of hierogamy, or *hieros gamos* as you say. Sacred marriage. It's about renewing the Earth."

As I learned about *hieros gamos,* I noticed I no longer felt the separate energies of the other lives I'd incorporated. Until recently, I'd been able to think about one of my other lives and feel its distinct energy—the personality of that life. But after my trip to Australia, I had no sense of the individual energies. It seemed odd to me. Why had I lost that ability? Or had I? Would it come back? As you might imagine, I simply didn't know and I wasn't getting any help from my so-called help.

"Easy," M said.

A few days later, Ramona finished up my weekly massage and asked whether I'd like to hear what she'd heard while working on my hamstrings.

"Of course," I said.

"I opened something for you. I did a lot of work around your heart."

"That's no surprise. The thing's hard to keep open."

"So I noticed," she said, "but this was different. Something new is opening for you."

"Like what?"

"I don't know," she said.

"Imagine that," I said.

"Easy," M said.

That evening I took a long walk after dinner and went to bed early. As I lay down my entire body started vibrating intensely. That wasn't unusual. I'd had similar experiences with other energy adjustments, but this was different. The vibrating didn't stop. It went on and on. All I could do was lie there and let whatever was happening happen, so I didn't fight it but it wore me out. Sometime after midnight I fell asleep from exhaustion and slept fitfully, waking what seemed like every few minutes to feel miserable for a while and go back to sleep. When I woke the next morning, I was a wreck. Luckily, I was going to see Sandy first thing.

"You look terrible," she said.

"There's a good reason for that."

"I heard before you came, you're going through a big shift, Steve. I've never seen one affect you like this."

Once again, I lay on Sandy's treatment table. She worked quietly on my feet while I whined about my awful night. She didn't seem to be listening.

"I see," she said, somewhere in the middle of one of my sentences.

"See what?" I asked.

"Oh, sorry, I wasn't listening …

"Probably a good thing. See what?" I asked again.

"Your other lives. The energies of those lives. They're all one energy in you now. They've been combined. You carry the energies of nine lives as one now. In this life as Steve. That's what happened during the night and they show me now you are becoming a white tree, energetically and metaphorically I think. Your branches reach into the sky beyond what I can see and your roots are growing deep into the Earth. I'm helping with grounding now. I've never seen anything like this. Such interesting things happen for you. They say you are the white tree. Giving and receiving. Bringing new, renewing energies to the Earth and receiving nourishment from the Earth. This is quite amazing."

"I heard that—about becoming the white tree—several years ago," I said. "But I didn't understand it and forgot about it till now."

"They say you'll feel better in a few days. Let this settle. More rest for you, I think."

Sandy was right. For the next several days, I slept like a log. (Sorry about that.) And napped 3 or 4 times every day. There was nothing intentional about the napping. I simply fell asleep in the middle of whatever I was doing. I had flashbacks of my grandfather. He was famous for his ability to nod off.

"You enjoy ever greater clarity," M said.

"About what?" I asked.

"Your partnership with the feminine – your sacred marriage. You've experienced the power of this union in different ways now. With Sandy and the joining of your energies, you bring this magnificent gift to the Earth. And having assimilated the energies of your other lives, your masculine energy comes to fullness. You are the white tree.

"Now you walk on. There will soon be another celebration – the celebration you've anticipated for some time now. A reunion."

"Ah, my dream. The one about the train. I still see it all so clearly in my head."

"Yes."

"The woman on the train. We were going to a celebration. And now you say it's a reunion? With whom?"

Laughter and clapping broke out among the Gathering. M ignored my question except to say, "Part of your adventure. Trust your knowing. We see you've purchased train tickets."

Yes, two round trip tickets to Pitlochry."

"Good," M said.

And then just 10 days before my Scotland trip, I was back on Sandy's table (every other week, as regular as clockwork). We talked about clarity – trying to make sense out of what had happened.

"Why the extra train ticket?" Sandy asked.

"I don't know for sure, but you remember my dream about the train and the woman on the train and the celebration?"

"Yes," Sandy said. "I thought the train was in Germany."

"That's what I thought at the time."

"The woman on the train. Her energy was familiar to you. You felt comfortable with her like you knew her."

"Right. And now I've bought two tickets on a train to Pitlochry in Scotland—not Germany—one for me and one for someone else, but I'm traveling to Scotland solo. So I don't know what's coming. For some reason that dream keeps popping into my head. Maybe it's relevant. Or not. We'll see."

"Will you take my Druid wood?"

"I'm told I don't need it. Remember the Earth blessing we did in Australia, when we danced?"

"Yes."

"We had no need of talismans. We don't need them any longer. I'll take my clamshell because I always take my clamshell, but your Druid wood is safer here. You won't have to worry about my losing it."

"I wasn't really worried about it…well, maybe just a little," she smiled.

⊷═◉ ◉═⊶

Later that day, I sat on the daybed in the cottage thumbing through an old journal. Sandy had healed me—again. I'd run my errands, breathed through my yoga as best I could, packed my bag, and now, once again, I was waiting—waiting this time for a trip to Scotland—and wondering about sacred marriage, Earth blessings, and the extra train ticket.

"Allow me to come to you," M suddenly said.

"You're coming…"

"Allow me to come to you. I will. A blanket waits for us in the grass under the tree at the top of the next hill."

M laughed. The Gathering cheered.

"The reunion. You mean…"

"Yes," M said.

"Your energy. A reincarnation of your energy?"

"Close enough," M said.

"Really? A real, honest-to-goodness, actual woman with a real body and…"

"Easy," M said.

Gradually the cottage returned to silence. Outside, the sun was high and hot in a light blue sky. An orchid on the bench by the window leaned toward the light, heavy with new buds. Gnawing nervously on a piece of tree bark, a squirrel peered in through the cottage door at me briefly and scurried away.

I sat—looking around the room and remembering. Marveling at the events of the last seven years. The mystery. So much I'd never have imagined. The extraordinary beauty of it all. And now a reunion. Would that happen in Scotland? Would I meet someone there? Or elsewhere? And when? Was she somebody I knew? Or someone new? I had a lot of questions. The thought of meeting someone in some unknown but pre-arranged way was inviting.

Something caught my eye in the garden. A bright red cardinal bobbed on a spindly twig in the plum tree above the stone walk that silently winds its way through scattered pine needle mulch and sprawling St. John's wort. A light breeze played with wind chimes on the porch while shadows of maple leaves danced on the wall by the window.

Dust motes floated around me in flickering strands of sunlight.

"Mo' to come child," Sarah said quietly. "We jus' gettin' started. God got da pen. He doin' da writin'. You doin' da livin'."

Keep walking, though there's no place to get to.
Don't try to see through the distances.
That's not for human beings.
Move within, but don't move the way fear makes you move.

—Rumi

Afterthought

AFTER I WROTE this book, I shared it with family and some friends. As you might imagine, reactions varied: silence, amazement, curiosity, disbelief, avoidance, jealousy, enthusiasm, etc. Responses were all over the place.

Several people asked essentially the same question: What do you *do* to connect with God and your helpers?

You may have noticed as you read the book that I was mostly surprised by what happened along the way. I didn't see much order in things. It's only in hindsight that I noticed the gradual evolution of *practices* that help me connect. I've listed them below. (They're all in the book, so this is just a summary of what you've read.) If you find these helpful, great. If not, that's fine too. Our paths are different so it wouldn't be surprising if evolving *practices* differed among us.

That said, here you go:

Saying yes was the start for me—feeling there was something more to this life (without knowing what it was), saying *yes* to it, and *stepping forward* through my fear into the unknown. Even with Sarah's loving encouragement, it was a gut-wrenchingly difficult *yes* for me.

Going on a pilgrimage. My trip to Brazil was pivotal. I didn't see it at the time, but a great deal changed for me after that trip.

Asking for help and trusting that I'll get the help I need. It's usually different from the help I want and it's rarely apparent to me until sometime after I've received it.

Noticing my fears and examining them. Is there really anything to fear? Most of the time, the answer is no. I can step forward without fear. Aware but not afraid.

Welcoming challenges. Challenges show me my fears so I can see them and, instead of responding the way fear wants me to respond, respond with love. Challenges offer me the opportunity to exercise my *personal response-ability.*

Doing creative things has been incredibly helpful and I now know creative opportunities are everywhere. I've enjoyed painting and writing and dancing. I've also enjoyed preparing a colorful salad and tending a garden and chatting with the lady at the cash register and folding a bath towel.

Writing in my journal, first thing in the morning nearly every day, recording my thoughts and whatever I hear, or think I hear, unfiltered.

Being still, which for me happens best when I'm not still. I'm not good at sitting in the lotus position with the hint of a smile on my face. Stillness happens for me while I'm walking, or sitting on my front porch drinking a cup of coffee, or washing a dish, or any other time I'm simply noticing what's right in front of me, letting my mind go quiet—not thinking about anything but what's in front of me.

Paying attention to my dreams and daydreams and asking what they want to show me. I found a dream coach helpful until I got the hang of it.

Receiving the healing touch of another – whether a professional or a friend. All that's needed is a peaceful environment and the loving touch of another. I give and receive a lot of healing touching. *Where two or more are gathered...the laying on of hands...*

Noticing energies—mostly sensations that feel electrical, sometimes subtle and sometimes intense. Sometimes a hazy color around another person (or thing) or a scent or a faint sound. Energies are always showing me something.

Listening to the loving voices. God and the Gathering never tell me what to do or insist on anything. They occasionally make suggestions and they're always coming up with interesting questions. The loving voices are easy to pick out of the noise.

Noticing coincidences. I used to dismiss them. Not anymore.

Checking in with my heart. More and more, I follow my heart and what it wants. I'm more spontaneous and much more willing to go.

Cultivating joy and gratitude. I'm far more loving, open and connected to God and the Gathering when I'm feeling *up*.

Allowing—doing my part as gracefully as I can and *allowing* the rest to come.

I'll leave it there even though I love making and revising a list. Looking it over now, I see that, for me, everything seems to have followed from saying *yes*. *Saying yes* and *stepping forward* were all that was needed. That was my way of handing God the pen. The rest, including these *practices*, simply came along when needed.